ON HEALTH AND LONG LIFE:
A Conversation

On Health
———— AND ————
Long Life
A Conversation

DAISAKU IKEDA

World Tribune Press

Published by World Tribune Press
A division of the SGI-USA
606 Wilshire Blvd., Santa Monica, CA 90401

© 2016 Soka Gakkai.
All rights reserved.
Printed in the United States of America.

Cover and interior design by Gopa & Ted2, Inc.

21 20 19 18 17   2 3 4 5 6 7

ISBN: 978-1-944604-01-1

LCCN: 2016944725

Table of Contents

Editor's Note	vii
CHAPTER 1: Learning From Illness	1
CHAPTER 2: Buddhism and Medicine	15
CHAPTER 3: The Influenza Mystery	25
CHAPTER 4: Are Our Lives Determined by Our Genes?	41
CHAPTER 5: Children and Stress	57
CHAPTER 6: A Constructive Approach to Aging	73
CHAPTER 7: "We Will Find Perpetual Youth"	89
CHAPTER 8: Dealing With Dementia	103
CHAPTER 9: The Key to Good Health Care	125
CHAPTER 10: The Human Touch	137
Notes	151
Index	155

Editor's Note

In *On Health and Long Life*, SGI President Ikeda once again takes up the all-important issues of birth, aging, sickness, and death. The conversations—held with doctors and nurses from Japan, the United States, and Malaysia—explore Buddhist insights and practical medical knowledge to provide the reader useful information to lead a long and fulfilling life. This series of dialogues first ran in the *Seikyo Shimbun*, the Soka Gakkai's daily newspaper in Japan, from 2005–06 under the title "Discussions on Life and Death."

The citations most commonly used in this book have been abbreviated as follows:

- **LSOC**, page number(s) refers to *The Lotus Sutra and Its Opening and Closing Sutras*, translated by Burton Watson (Tokyo: Soka Gakkai, 2009).

- **OTT**, page number(s) refers to *The Record of the Orally Transmitted Teachings*, translated by Burton Watson (Tokyo: Soka Gakkai, 2004).

- **WND**, page number(s) refers to *The Writings of Nichiren Daishonin*, vol. 1 (WND-1) (Tokyo, Soka Gakkai, 1999) and vol. 2 (WND-2) (Tokyo: Soka Gakkai, 2006).

1: Learning From Illness

SGI PRESIDENT IKEDA: Making the twenty-first century a century of life—this was a central theme of my dialogue with Dr. Linus Pauling (1901–94), an eminent American scientist and the recipient of Nobel Prizes in chemistry and peace. In our discussions, he described a century of life as "a century in which greater attention will be paid to human beings and their happiness and health."[1] This has indeed become the focus of the present age.

DR. SHOSAKU NARUMI[2]**:** The ethical implications of new medical technologies that challenge the very definition of life—organ transplants, in vitro fertilization, gene therapy, and cloning—have become an extremely important subject of discussion today. Moreover, there is a growing focus among people on health and how to live a long and fulfilling life.

DR. CHIAKI NISHIYAMA[3]**:** According to a recent *Yomiuri Shimbun* survey (October 28, 2005), books on such subjects as health, medicine, welfare, and pensions are the most popular with Japanese readers today. This clearly reflects the concerns of a graying population.

DR. YOICHI UEHIGASHI[4]**:** Government statistics indicate that this year (2005), the total number of Japanese ages sixty-five and over now encompasses 20 percent of the population. In ten years, one in four Japanese will be in this category.

IKEDA: In addition to improvements in diet and sanitation, advances in medicine have contributed greatly to this trend.

NARUMI: But with an aging population also come the issues of medically assisted death and the right to die with dignity. As average life expectancy increases, the more crucial it becomes to find ways to spend the final chapter of our lives in a healthy and fulfilling way. For these reasons, humankind is being forced to face fundamental questions about death and what it means to lead a genuinely meaningful life.

IKEDA: Birth, aging, sickness, and death—these are the inescapable realities of life. They are the most pressing issues in life and eternal questions facing humanity. I have already discussed Buddhism and life, health, and medicine from many different perspectives, but the fact is that these issues are the central themes of our time and examining them is becoming increasingly important. I would therefore like to take this opportunity to discuss them more deeply with members of the doctors division, who play such a pivotal role in this century of health and life.

NISHIYAMA, NARUMI, AND UEHIGASHI: We look forward to it.

NISHIYAMA: Confronting these issues with our patients on a daily basis, we also have many questions we'd like to ask you about the Buddhist perspective on birth, aging, sickness, and death.

IKEDA: Please ask anything you'd like. Let's conduct this discussion in an informal, relaxed manner—not like a lecture, but as if we were taking a stroll together down a tree-lined avenue.

Shakyamuni's Lesson for a Grieving Mother

IKEDA: One of the Buddhist scriptures tells the story of a woman who lost her beloved child to illness. Distraught with grief, she carried her child's little body through the city, begging everyone she met to give her some medicine that would bring her child back to life.

One of those to whom she spoke took pity on her and told her to go visit Shakyamuni. When she presented herself before the Buddha, he said that he had something that would cure her child. He then instructed her to go into town and collect a pinch of white mustard seed from any home there. The only condition was that the mustard seed must come from a house in which there had never been a death.

The mother hurried back to the town and went from door to door asking for the mustard seed. She was determined to find it no matter what. But of course, there was no house in the entire city in which no one had died.

Eventually, she understood: death comes to everyone. She was not alone in her sorrow. And so she became a follower of Shakyamuni.[5]

UEHIGASHI: Shakyamuni wished to impart the message to her that she was not the only mother to lose a child. Most people had in fact experienced the death of a loved one, but had overcome their grief to go on living.

IKEDA: How should we lead our lives, impermanent and constantly changing as they are, in such a way as to transform them into existences of eternity, happiness, true self, and purity? This question was the starting point of Shakyamuni's quest, and it is the challenge of Buddhism to answer it.

The core issues of birth, aging, sickness, and death are

therefore the main focus of Buddhism, which teaches a way to fundamentally resolve the problems presented therein.

All Existence Undergoes the Eternal Cycle of Birth and Death

Narumi: The inexorable law of birth, aging, sickness, and death is not restricted to human beings.

Ikeda: Plants, animals, and all things existing in the universe undergo these four stages, following a cycle of formation, continuance, decline, and disintegration. Birth, aging, sickness, and death are not simply a problem for the individual; they are issues that affect all existence at the most fundamental level. In that sense, when we speak of creating a century of life and health, we are also speaking of creating a century of the earth and the universe.

Furthermore, as Nichiren writes, "No phenomena—either heaven or earth, yin or yang, the sun or the moon, the five planets, or any of the worlds from hell to Buddhahood—are free from the two phases of life and death" (WND-1, 216). Buddhism views birth, aging, sickness, and death from many perspectives—not only on the level of the individual, but also on the cosmic level, and across the three existences of past, present, and future.

Uehigashi: The renowned British astronomer Sir Fred Hoyle (1915–2001), with whom you engaged in a dialogue (in 1991), also noted that there are two perspectives on the birth, growth, and death of the universe. Some believe that this process takes place just once, while others hold that it is a repeating cycle.

The Women's Perspective on Health Is Indispensable

Ikeda: If I may change the subject, I have heard, Dr. Nishiyama, that your father and grandfather were both physicians. Your grandfather, I understand, ran a private practice in Hiroshima, where he treated many of the victims of the atomic bomb.

Nishiyama: Yes. I was five at the time. My grandfather didn't want me to see the terrible condition of the patients, so he forbade me to go to his office. But one day I snuck a peek at the patients waiting for treatment in the courtyard separating the main building and the examination room. They all sat there with dazed expressions. I felt I had seen something I shouldn't have, and I suddenly grew very afraid.

I have never forgotten that scene, which is probably the reason I decided to enter the field of medicine.

Ikeda: You became the first doctors division women's leader this year [2005], Dr. Nishiyama. Women are playing an increasingly important role in every arena in society. The perspective of women is particularly indispensable with regard to the century of health. I hope you will do your best.

Dr. Narumi, have you had any personal death-related experience?

Narumi: When I was a junior high school student, I was suspected of having a bone infection, and I had an operation on my arm. That was the first time I ever thought seriously about death.

After that, I entered Soka High School, where I learned from you, the school's founder, the importance of devoting oneself to something for ten years and gaining mastery in it. Making this my personal guideline, I gave my all to my studies, resolved to contribute to society as a physician who cherishes and cares for each patient.

Since becoming a doctor, I have felt it is my responsibility to help not only my patients but also their family members deal with the sufferings of birth, aging, sickness, and death.

IKEDA: Now as of November 2005, there are 310 Soka school alumni active in the field of medicine, including those still in medical school. Soka alumni are demonstrating great proof of victory in every area of society. As the schools' founder, nothing makes me happier or prouder.

The Importance of Doctor-Patient Communication

IKEDA: Dr. Uehigashi, you are in charge of the doctors division Health Counseling Center, aren't you?

UEHIGASHI: When the Soka Youth Physicians Conference was established in the doctors division twelve years ago (in 1993), we discussed what practical action we could take as physicians and came up with the idea of a Health Counseling Center. In the health field, good communication between physicians and patients is extremely important, but there are still many unresolved issues in this regard. Our aim was to help alleviate patients' worries and concerns and make a contribution to our communities and society at large.

IKEDA: In Buddhism, compassion means to free one from suffering and bring joy (see OTT, 173). It is important to listen to people's fears and problems about birth, aging, sickness, and death and respond sensitively, as well as to encourage them confidently. This is what it means to be a compassionate doctor, and I believe this is the mission of the doctors division.

UEHIGASHI: I will do my utmost to impart hope and comfort to my patients.

Devadatta's Jealousy

NISHIYAMA: Come to think of it, the Buddha is said to have "few ills and few worries" (LSOC, 254). I wonder if that means he never caught colds!

IKEDA: Apparently he did catch colds. There's a record of him having taken medicine for it. Once when Shakyamuni caught a cold, his physician, the great healer Jivaka, combined thirty-two different medicinal ingredients with refined milk and instructed Shakyamuni to take a dosage of about sixteen ounces per day.

NISHIYAMA: Jivaka is also known for having stood up to Devadatta.

IKEDA: That's true. He also remonstrated with King Ajatashatru, an oppressive ruler who was influenced by the cunning Devadatta.

Devadatta learned that Shakyamuni had received medicine from Jivaka, and, out of his sense of rivalry with Shakyamuni, he decided to do the same even though he wasn't sick. So he ordered Jivaka to prepare medicine for him as well. Devadatta was very arrogant and deeply envied Shakyamuni. Jivaka prepared the same medicine for Devadatta, but warned him to take only two ounces of it. Devadatta, however, was determined to take as much of the medicine as Shakyamuni had. Jivaka warned him that his body was different from Shakyamuni's, and he would suffer severe side effects if he took the larger dose.

But Devadatta would not be dissuaded and, declaring that his body was exactly like Shakyamuni's, took the same amount. He immediately felt sharp pains in his joints and fell ill. He was suffering so terribly that he screamed and writhed in agony.

NARUMI: The point of this episode, in my opinion, is not so much the importance of taking the prescribed dosage but to strictly reproach the evil of Devadatta's envy and arrogance.

IKEDA: I agree. The story continues that Shakyamuni then took pity on Devadatta's suffering and stroked his head. In an instant, the pain stopped and Devadatta felt better.

This anecdote reveals the extreme degree of Devadatta's envy of Shakyamuni. Second Soka Gakkai President Josei Toda often used to warn that Devadatta was ruled by jealousy and intense rivalry. In sad proof of this, Devadatta's response to Shakyamuni's aid was not to be grateful but to declare that he would study medicine himself and get his revenge.[6]

NISHIYAMA: Unfortunately, ingratitude and jealousy are not uncommon to our world today.

Never Underestimate the Symptoms of a Cold

IKEDA: Getting back to the subject of colds, they say that a cold may lead to all kinds of illnesses.

UEHIGASHI: In an ancient Chinese medical text, it is written: "Wind is the cause of many illnesses. Once it penetrates the body, its nature is dynamic and changeable, and it has many pathological manifestations."[7] That is probably the source of the belief that colds are the starting point of many other diseases.

NARUMI: "Wind" here refers to "pathogenic wind," the Chinese characters of which mean "cold" in Japanese. In traditional Chinese medicine, there are six external factors or conditions, such as certain types of climate, that are considered to lead to disease. One of these is pathogenic wind. Because this factor spreads quickly, like the wind, it is thought to combine readily with other pathogenic influences to contribute to the manifestation of many diseases.

IKEDA: I see. Thank you for explaining that.

UEHIGASHI: Colds can trigger other illnesses, such as pneumonia, myocarditis (inflammation of the heart muscle), and nephritis (inflammation of the kidneys). It's especially important to take care when we are weakened by a prolonged cold.

NISHIYAMA: Another danger is to mistake fever, cough, or other symptoms as indicating a cold when they might point to something more serious.

NARUMI: The first stages of pulmonary tuberculosis, lung cancer, pleurisy, collagen disease, acute kidney infection, influenza, and many other illnesses are also characterized by fever and cough.

IKEDA: In other words, we should never take cold symptoms too lightly.

UEHIGASHI: Doctors also need to be careful not to overlook other possibilities when examining patients with cold symptoms.

Sickness Shows Us What We Are

IKEDA: Nichiren writes, "If you try to treat someone's illness without knowing its cause, you will only make the person sicker than before" (WND-1, 774). Doctors bear a heavy responsibility. At the same time, we patients must also look after ourselves. When we catch a cold, it's important that we examine our lifestyle to identify why we caught it and find the ultimate cause.

UEHIGASHI: Lack of sleep and physical or mental exhaustion are believed to make us more susceptible to colds. Talking with people suffering from lifestyle-related diseases, I find that there is always some specific cause for their ailment.

NARUMI: In some cases, lack of self-control and discipline can manifest itself as poor diet, lack of exercise, and stress.

IKEDA: Lack of self-control and discipline always affect other aspects of one's life as well. That is why we mustn't treat our illnesses lightly. An old proverb says that sickness shows us what we are. Illness can be an important opportunity to examine our life and how we live it and to elevate our life condition.

NISHIYAMA: I think that illness can help you be more understanding and sympathetic about the limitations experienced by the physically weak and the elderly.

IKEDA: That's very true. Sickness can purify your heart and make you kinder. The French author Romain Rolland (1866–

1944) wrote: "Illness is often a blessing. By ravaging the body it frees the soul and purifies it."[8] Furthermore, those struggling against illness can deeply savor the joy of being alive.

UEHIGASHI: You struggled with illness as a youth, didn't you, President Ikeda?

IKEDA: I did. I was sickly from the time I was a child, and as a youth I suffered from tuberculosis. I was even told by a doctor that I probably wouldn't live past thirty. I was forced to face the reality of death at a very early age. But because I encountered Mr. Toda and gave my all to the lofty goal of kosen-rufu, I have been able to live a life of unparalleled fulfillment and complete engagement.

Suffering Makes Us Richer and Stronger

NISHIYAMA: You can build an indestructible spirit through the struggle against illness. I have learned this from observing many patients who are Soka Gakkai members. Though suffering from severe illnesses, they are always offering wholehearted encouragement to the other patients in their hospital room as well as the people who visit them.

IKEDA: That's so admirable. People who have devoted themselves to working for the welfare of others and society are always strong in a crisis. They have the courage and conviction to face sickness and death with calm composure. And those who fight against illness with the power of faith can elevate their life state even further. They can encourage others with tremendous resolve. That itself represents a triumph over illness.

The Austrian psychologist Viktor E. Frankl (1905–97) said,

"We mature in suffering, grow because of it—it makes us richer and stronger."[9]

NARUMI: The fact that Dr. Frankl was a Nazi concentration camp survivor gives his words extra weight.

IKEDA: Buddhism teaches that sufferings are the fuel or springboard to enlightenment. Life is filled with problems. Our problems and sufferings lead us to chant Nam-myoho-renge-kyo to the Gohonzon. If we chant, make efforts, and grow, our hearts will become richer and stronger. Suffering is the fuel of wisdom, and it opens the way to happiness.

This applies to the suffering of illness as well. Through sickness, human beings can gain insight into the meaning of life, understand life's value and dignity, and enjoy a more fulfilling existence.

Nichiren writes, "Illness gives rise to the resolve to attain the way" (WND-1, 937). The suffering of illness leads to enlightenment, and the hindrance of illness is a "good friend." Through the power of the Mystic Law, we can transform suffering into joy, anxiety into hope, worries into peace of mind, and every difficulty into a positive outcome. Furthermore, the strong life force and wisdom we acquire through chanting makes it possible for us to win over illness.

NISHIYAMA: I know that to be true, having seen with my own eyes numerous cases of patients who have recovered from illness through the power of faith.

IKEDA: We should never think that illness is a kind of failure or reason for embarrassment. It is not a sign of misfortune or defeat. Through our Buddhist practice, we can transform illness into proof of our victory in life. And the protection we receive will extend to our entire family and all our relations. Such is the unfathomable power of the Mystic Law.

How do we overcome the sufferings and anxieties of old age? How do we establish a life state of eternity, happiness, true self, and purity that cannot be shaken by sickness or death? In the twenty-first century, people are increasingly seeking a correct philosophy of life and death and view of human existence.

UEHIGASHI: Conscientious doctors have begun to earnestly explore these philosophical and spiritual issues.

IKEDA: To meet the needs of the times and provide sound answers to these questions, I would like to invite young physicians and medical students to join us to discuss new ideas and perspectives.

Let us foster youthful talent as we vigorously and dynamically open the century of health.

2: Buddhism and Medicine

IKEDA: Nichiren tells the story of King Rinda's illness. When the king heard the "neighing of white horses," his health returned and "the strength of his body and the perceptive powers of his mind became many hundreds and thousands of times greater than they had been before" (WND-1, 986). Thus, he was able to take the lead again and work for the sake of his people.

The "neighing of white horses" is a metaphor for voices chanting Nam-myoho-renge-kyo. Our daily Buddhist practice, which involves doing gongyo and chanting Nam-myoho-renge-kyo morning and evening, is the best health regimen there is, for it puts our life in rhythm with the universe and greatly increases our vitality.

NARUMI: Medically speaking as well, gongyo is good for our health. By sitting up straight and using our voice, we improve the functions of our lungs and heart. The effect is the same whether we sit kneeling Japanese style or in a chair.

IKEDA: When we chant in a resounding voice, we unconsciously breathe from our abdomen. I've heard that's beneficial to our health. Is that correct?

NISHIYAMA: Slowly inhaling and exhaling from the abdomen stimulates the parasympathetic nervous system and has a relaxing and calming effect.

UEHIGASHI: This positively influences the entire body, improving circulation and warming the extremities. It also enhances the immune system and may aid cold prevention.

IKEDA: I see. So breathing out slowly as you chant is a healthy practice supported by medical data.

Plutarch (46–127 CE), whose *Parallel Lives* I read as a youth, said that speaking itself promotes good health. Using one's voice on a daily basis, he added, is a way to preserve one's health and increase one's strength.[10] He was talking about life force, not physical strength.

NARUMI: Chanting does indeed give rise to powerful life force.

Drive Out the Poisons

IKEDA: That's right. Nichiren states, "Taking the highly effective medicine of the Wonderful Law will relieve us of the sufferings inflicted by earthly desires, the three poisons of greed, anger, and foolishness" (OTT, 131). Nam-myoho-renge-kyo permeates our body with the best medicine there is. We should therefore chant in a way that is strong and invigorating, so as to drive all the poisons out of our body.

NISHIYAMA: Yet sometimes I see people who are so tired that they are falling asleep in front of the Gohonzon!

IKEDA: Nothing escapes a woman's sharp eye, does it?

The desire to chant even when one is tired is admirable, but the best way to do it is with one's eyes wide open, looking straight at the Gohonzon, and repeating Nam-myoho-renge-kyo with the vigorous rhythm of a horse galloping over open plains. If we chant with a sleepy countenance, our appearance, too, will always be listless and sleepy!

Disharmony of the Four Elements

UEHIGASHI: The weather has started getting colder. Does Buddhism recognize any connections between climate and health?

IKEDA: Nichiren writes about changes in the weather: "There is definitely something extraordinary in . . . the way in which summer, autumn, winter, and spring give way to each other" (WND-1, 637), and "Heat or cold . . . has no shape or form that the eye can see. Yet in winter the cold comes to attack the trees and grasses, humans and beasts, and in summer the heat comes to torment people and animals" (WND-1, 760).

Buddhism also teaches that changes in weather or the seasons can cause illness. For example, in *Great Concentration and Insight,* the Great Teacher T'ien-t'ai of China writes, "Cold assists the water element and impairs the fire element, leading to illness arising from the excess of the water element."

NISHIYAMA: He's referring to two of the four elements of traditional Eastern thought, isn't he?

IKEDA: Yes. In ancient India, it was believed that all living things were composed of four elements—earth, water, fire, and wind or air. The earth element is represented by our bones, hair, teeth, and muscles. Water is our blood and other bodily fluids, fire is our body temperature and the digestion process, and wind is our breath and metabolism. Human beings were regarded as consisting of a combination of these elements.

T'ien-t'ai states that illness occurs when these four elements are out of balance. In the above example, he is saying that as outdoor temperatures drop, the balance of the fire and water elements is disrupted, opening the door for illness.

UEHIGASHI: In modern medical terms, imbalances in the autonomic nervous system and hormone levels, as well as lowered resistance to disease, can also be thought of as stemming from disharmony of the four elements. This allows viruses to attack the body and causes colds or other illnesses.

SIX CAUSES OF ILLNESS

IKEDA: In addition to "disharmony of the four elements," T'ien-t'ai identified five other causes of illness (WND-1, 631). The second he mentions is "improper eating or drinking," and the third is "inappropriate practice of seated meditation," which includes the inability to concentrate, laziness, and leading an unbalanced life lacking adequate sleep or exercise.

NARUMI: Having a proper diet, getting enough sleep and exercise, and keeping a regular schedule—things that you are always encouraging members to do, President Ikeda—are extremely important.

IKEDA: The fourth cause of illness noted by T'ien-t'ai is "attack by demons," which refers to illness caused by external factors.

UEHIGASHI: In medical terms, this would be such things as viruses, bacteria, and allergens. Emotional stress could also be regarded as belonging to this category, I think.

IKEDA: The fifth cause is "the work of devils." This refers to internal factors such as greed or other uncontrolled impulses disrupting the healthy operation of the body and mind and harming one's health.

NISHIYAMA: Today, all kinds of mental illnesses are on the rise.

IKEDA: And the sixth cause of illness is "the effects of karma." This refers to illnesses occurring as a result of negative karma created in this and former existences. This cause is based on a Buddhist viewpoint, and the Mystic Law is the fundamental means for overcoming it.

In reality, of course, illnesses are the result of the complex interaction of many or all of these causes.

THE "HIGHLY EFFECTIVE MEDICINE" OF THE MYSTIC LAW

UEHIGASHI: Listening to your explanation, Buddhism and medicine are clearly more interrelated than we might imagine. In fact, many Buddhas and bodhisattvas are described in Buddhist texts as physicians, and the word *medicine* appears in the names of several of them.

IKEDA: Yes, that's true. As I mentioned earlier, the Mystic Law is often referred to as the "highly effective medicine" that has the power to purify and rejuvenate life. The Buddha was also known as the "king of physicians," because just as a doctor provides appropriate treatment according to the symptoms of his patient, the Buddha knows the best way to treat the sufferings afflicting all living beings.

There is also Bodhisattva Medicine King, who heals people's direst illnesses and relieves them of suffering. I regard the members of the doctors division and nurses groups as manifestations of Bodhisattva Medicine King.

UEHIGASHI: Buddhism seems to have a high regard for the art of medicine.

IKEDA: Nichiren also had a considerable degree of medical knowledge. He wrote, for example, "To illustrate, a person has five internal organs [heart, lungs, liver, kidneys, and spleen] but should even one of them become diseased, it will infect all the others, and eventually the person will die" (WND-1, 1026).

NARUMI: And, of course, that's true. We know that people with weak hearts can have lung and liver ailments due to poor circulation, while those suffering from kidney problems can have high blood pressure and suffer from heart problems and anemia.

IKEDA: Nichiren was also aware of the importance of being circumspect when prescribing medicine. He writes, "A skilled physician, for example, may discern the causes of all kinds of illnesses as well as the relative efficacy of various medicines, but nevertheless refrains from indiscriminately applying the most powerful medicine and instead employs other medicines, depending upon the nature of the illness" (WND-1, 669).

NISHIYAMA: It's really amazing. Nichiren's writings are filled with fascinating passages that still hold true today.

Buddhism Values the Art of Medicine

IKEDA: Buddhism values the art of medicine. This was true of Shakyamuni, T'ien-t'ai, and Nichiren alike. Nichiren states, "Just as one searches out some potent medicine when one is attempting to cure a critical illness . . ." (WND-2, 540).

NISHIYAMA: When Nichiren suffered from illness, he was treated by his disciple Shijo Kingo, who was a physician.

IKEDA: He writes gratefully that Shijo Kingo treated his diarrhea (see WND-2, 754), and on another occasion, he advises a female disciple to seek treatment for her illness from Shijo Kingo (see WND-1, 955).

NARUMI: I have heard that people used to think it was a sign of weak faith to consult a doctor.

IKEDA: Receiving proper medical treatment has absolutely nothing to do with the strength of one's faith. Nichiren writes, "Early treatment by a skilled physician can cure even serious illnesses, not to mention minor ones" (WND-1, 954). Referring to this passage, President Toda used to say that anyone with an illness that could be treated by a doctor should seek medical help.

Treating illness is a doctor's job. The function of faith is to strengthen our life force, which can aid with healing. It's a mistake to confuse the two.

First Soka Gakkai President Tsunesaburo Makiguchi also said that overcoming illness comes down to a combination of the patient's own life force and the doctor's ability as a medical professional.

Buddhism is reason. If we have symptoms of an illness, we should seek treatment right away. In fact, precisely because we are practicing Nichiren Buddhism, we need to take every precaution to preserve our health. It stands to reason that we should wisely make use of the available medical treatment so that it serves us in the most valuable way.

NISHIYAMA: Many people have actually saved their own lives by detecting their symptoms early on and seeking immediate treatment.

NARUMI: It's also crucial to listen to one's doctors and follow their advice. People should neither try to tough it out nor avoid seeing a doctor out of a fear of what they might find; rather, they should make good use of the medical facilities available to them.

Becoming Your Own Doctor and Nurse

IKEDA: The important thing is to have wisdom. The Buddhist scriptures teach that wisdom is the key. For example, *The Great Canon of Monastic Rules* states, "Exert yourself and be wise." In other words, we must act wisely, sparing no effort in trying to regain our health.

NARUMI: That is certainly good advice.

IKEDA: Recently, there has been talk of physician-induced, or iatrogenic, disease, hasn't there?

NARUMI: This is a concept put forth by the Austrian philosopher Ivan Illich (1926–2002) referring to illnesses caused by doctors and medical treatment, such as through mistaken drug prescriptions, medical malpractice, or overly aggressive or invasive medical treatment.

IKEDA: Illich warned people against losing their autonomy and relying too heavily on medical science or doctors. Japanese people, in particular, tend to leave everything up to the doctor.

NISHIYAMA: While doctors are responsible for diagnosing patients' illnesses and suggesting treatment, it is ultimately up to patients to decide whether to follow that treatment, to take their medications, and to watch their diet.

IKEDA: The point is that we mustn't be passive with regard to our treatment but take an active role in it. In the end, we are our own chief physician and head nurse.

As Japanese society continues to age, it is clear that the country's current policies for medical insurance and assisted care are insufficient. All of us are thus going to need the wisdom and the determination to take responsibility for our own health to a certain degree. The founder of modern nursing, Florence Nightingale (1820–1910), said that wisdom is the ability to put knowledge to use in the real world.

A Creative Life Contributes to Health

NARUMI: I also think it's very important to have the resolve not to be defeated by slight illnesses or a poor condition.

IKEDA: That's right. Nichiren's disciple Sairen-bo wished to retreat to the mountains because of the illness he was battling. While conveying his deep sympathy with Sairen-bo's struggle, Nichiren writes to him, "But if you should for a time retire to a dwelling in the mountain valleys, once your illness is mended and conditions are favorable again, you should set aside thoughts of personal well-being and devote yourself to the propagation of the teachings" (WND-2, 460).

NISHIYAMA: Nichiren was very concerned about the health of his followers and gave his all to encouraging them.

IKEDA: But he didn't encourage only their recuperation. Rather, he urged them to win out over illness, regain their health, and continue striving with all their might for the sake of the Law, the welfare of others, and society as long as they lived. His encouragement is at once compassionate and stern.

If you allow your fighting spirit to wane because of illness, your life itself will become ill and you will not be able to bring it to a splendid close.

NARUMI: I agree completely. Buddhism is concerned with winning, and so is health.

IKEDA: I have published a dialogue with the noted bioethicist Dr. Guy Bourgeault of the University of Montreal, Canada.

UEHIGASHI: Yes, Dr. René Simard, the renowned cancer expert and former rector of the same university, also took part in that dialogue, didn't he?

IKEDA: That's right. During our talk, Dr. Bourgeault stated that health is not the mere absence of illness. It is not a static state, he said, but "the tension between a precarious equilibrium and the constant dynamic of its re-establishment."[11] What this means, in other words, is that we need to challenge ourselves throughout our life. We should strive to create something, to continue moving forward, constantly opening new paths of development. Such a creative existence is, I think, the dynamism of which Dr. Bourgeault speaks. It also represents a genuinely healthy state of being.

Nichiren declares: "Nam-myoho-renge-kyo is like the roar of a lion. What sickness can therefore be an obstacle?" (WND-1, 412). We must keep advancing, triumphing over all manner of illness and pressing onward. It is by facing every obstacle with earnest, all-out prayer and firm, unwavering determination that we can enjoy a life shining with true health.

3: The Influenza Mystery

IKEDA: With the arrival of winter, people living in cold and snowy areas have a lot to put up with. I've heard that the average January temperature of the Sakha Republic (Yakutia), 40 percent of which lies within the Arctic Circle, is fifty-eight degrees below zero Fahrenheit. It's so cold that your breath freezes and you can hear it crackling. They call the sound "the whispering of the stars."

NARUMI: At those temperatures, even viruses that thrive in cold, dry conditions are inactivated, so the people there must be free from colds and influenza.

IKEDA: That's true. When I met Sakha Minister of Culture Andrei S. Borisov last year (January 2004), he said that his people don't mind the harsh cold of winter, remarking with a smile that they regard it as very hygienic. A proud Sakha maxim states that the extreme cold is a friend to the courageous.

NISHIYAMA: That's a good saying. We need to have courage to withstand the winter's cold.

IKEDA: Speaking of influenza, there's increasing concern in the international community about the possibility of a new influenza outbreak, isn't there?

NARUMI: Yes. Last month (November 2005), a conference of specialists was held at the headquarters of the World Health Organization in Geneva. At the conference, WHO Director-General Lee Jong-wook warned that it is only a matter of time before a new influenza virus strikes human populations.

IKEDA: What precisely is influenza? How is it different from an ordinary cold? People talk about influenza, but I wonder how many really know what it is. Why don't we begin our discussion here?

NISHIYAMA: Yes, that's a good starting point. From today, Dr. Ryuto Hirasawa, Tokyo No. 2 Area doctors division secretary, will be joining us. Welcome.

DR. RYUTO HIRASAWA: Thank you. I'm glad to be here.

IKEDA: Dr. Hirasawa, you're a Tokyo Soka schools graduate, aren't you? As the schools' founder, I'd like to thank you for your constant advice regarding the health of all Soka school students.

HIRASAWA: I know how precious the students are to you, President Ikeda. I will continue to do my very best to look after them.

Different From a Cold

IKEDA: What is the meaning of the word *influenza*?

HIRASAWA: It comes from the Italian word for *influence*. In medieval Italy, it was believed that influenza was caused by the influence of the stars.

Ikeda: It seems the people of those times believed that stars had mystical powers.

Hirasawa: That's correct. They also calculated when the next influenza outbreak would occur according to the movements of the stars.

Ikeda: How is influenza different from a cold?

Nishiyama: The viruses that cause them are different, and the symptoms of influenza are more serious. In many cases, influenza causes a sudden fever of more than one hundred degrees Fahrenheit, headaches, and aching joints and muscles.

Narumi: Another characteristic of influenza, or the flu as it is commonly called, is that it is highly contagious. It can spread through an entire family, and its outbreak in schools can result in the cancellation of classes.

Flu Shots and Vaccines

Ikeda: What steps are taken to prevent it from spreading at the Soka schools?

Hirasawa: We encourage parents to have their children vaccinated prior to flu season. This is completely voluntary, though.

Ikeda: I've heard that fewer people in Japan get flu shots than in the West.

Nishiyama: Yes, that's true. This fact seems to stem from the doubts people held about the effectiveness of the mass vaccination of all elementary and junior high school students that was conducted in Japan in the past.

Hirasawa: Of course, there are limits to the protection a vaccine can provide. Vaccination can't prevent every infection and outbreak. But given the increase in influenza outbreaks here in Japan and overseas in recent years, I think it is a mistake to ignore the positive effects of vaccinations.

Ikeda: I see. In the West, influenza is known as a killer of the elderly. Older people, whose immune systems are not as strong as when they were younger, need to take special care.

Narumi: The older you are, the worse your symptoms are likely to be, so I recommend vaccinations for the elderly. Research has shown that vaccination can reduce the chance of catching the flu by about 45 percent in healthy individuals over sixty-five, and reduces deaths from the flu by about 80 percent.

Nishiyama: The vaccine takes approximately two weeks to become effective. In most years, the flu season in Japan starts in mid-December and continues through the beginning of March, so it's good to get your flu shot early.

Narumi: It should be noted, however, that those with an allergic reaction to eggs need to consult their doctor before receiving the vaccine, which is grown in eggs.

Fresh Air and Sufficient Humidity

Ikeda: Are there any other steps you suggest to prevent catching the flu?

Hirasawa: In schools, we suggest opening the classroom windows during break time to bring in fresh air. The virus is also inhibited by humidity, so it's good to have a humidifier running in places where people tend to gather.

IKEDA: Careful consideration is important. Schools are citadels where the important work of educating people takes place, where the precious leaders of the future are fostered. As such, they must be places of complete safety and health.

HIRASAWA: We also encourage students to get sufficient rest, nutrition, and sleep, and to wash their hands and gargle regularly.

NISHIYAMA: We all should make it a practice to wash our hands thoroughly with soap when we come in from outdoors.

IKEDA: In spite of how simple and fundamental these preventative steps are, it's surprising how few of us employ them. We should also make them a part of our strategy in the prevention of ordinary colds.

Painstaking Care and Prompt Encouragement

NARUMI: I have heard that Shakyamuni also advised his followers about matters of hygiene such as washing their hands and rinsing their mouths.

IKEDA: That's correct. The Buddhist scriptures go into considerable detail about such matters, indicating how important they were regarded.

A mentor prays and thinks sincerely about how to ensure that his disciples stay well and can carry out their Buddhist practice in sound health.

NISHIYAMA: Buddhist compassion is manifested in concrete behavior.

IKEDA: Nichiren Daishonin also concerned himself deeply with the health of each of his disciples and whenever one fell ill, he was quick to write a letter or send a message of encouragement. In one letter, he writes:

> When someone reported to me, however, that you had been taken with this illness, day and night, morning and evening I addressed the Lotus Sutra on the matter, morning and evening I implored the gods of the blue heavens. And now today I have received word that you have recovered from illness. Could any tidings be more joyful than these? (WND-2, 1034)

True leaders go to great lengths to enable others to advance along the pathway toward happiness and experience a life of fulfillment. They also respond immediately to the reports they receive. Prompt action imparts courage and hope to others.

HIRASAWA: You have taken the lead in demonstrating the essence of such humanism in Soka education, President Ikeda.

Facing the Death of Patients

IKEDA: I'm curious to know what your thoughts were the first time you had to face the death of a patient.

NARUMI: My first experience with the death of a patient was when I was an intern. A middle-aged female patient died of a cerebral hemorrhage. My first thoughts were whether I had correctly understood her condition and treated her properly and sufficiently. There are cases in which the physician's ability can mean the difference between life and death. Realizing that, I resolved to constantly strive to improve as a physician.

IKEDA: I understand your feelings. Were you the one who informed the patient's family members of her death?

NARUMI: Yes. I felt it no small burden that it was up to me as the doctor to make the medical determination of death. I also questioned whether my patient had been fortunate to have had me as her physician in her final moments.

IKEDA: That's a very profound starting point. How about you, Dr. Hirasawa?

HIRASAWA: I was an intern, too, when I first experienced the death of a patient. He had a malignant tumor in his intestine and died just a few days after coming under my care. The supervising doctor confirmed his death, using a stethoscope, taking his pulse, and checking that the cardiac monitor showed no activity. I stood by watching, unable to do anything. I remember going home that day with a hollow feeling at how quickly death comes.

NISHIYAMA: I felt the same way. Since I'm a dermatologist, few of my patients are actually facing life-threatening illnesses. But during my third year as a physician, I first witnessed death—and in fact I lost three patients in one night. They were all in critical conditions, suffering from diabetes and terminal cancer. Not only was it the first time in my adult life to see death but also to inform the family. I was so upset by the experience that I don't remember anything other than telling the family of their loss.

A Society in Denial About Death

IKEDA: Your experiences are all very sobering.

What do you say to families when a loved one dies? Is there anything you say to encourage them?

NARUMI: In an effort to lessen the shock as much as possible, I try to keep the family well informed about the patient's condition and prognosis throughout the illness.

HIRASAWA: But I think the only thing you can really do is stand by quietly with the family and watch over the patient's last moments. You have to wait for the family to fully accept the fact that their loved one has indeed passed away.

NISHIYAMA: The most difficult thing is when the family is unable to accept the death. In such cases, we must do our best to encourage the family in any way we can.

IKEDA: I see. Death is the fundamental issue of existence. It is an inescapable reality for us all, but today many people seem to have forgotten that—or rather, they are in active denial of this truth. That's why they find it so difficult to deal with death when at last they are forced to face it.

Nichiren writes:

> Having received life, one cannot escape death. Yet though everyone, from the noblest, the emperor, on down to the lowliest commoner, recognizes this as a fact, not even one person in a thousand or ten thousand truly takes the matter seriously or grieves over it. (WND-1, 99)

HIRASAWA: This is very true.

IKEDA: That's why a philosophy that addresses the matter of life and death and enables us to live in the most correct way is so necessary. This is an important point not only for us as individuals but for society as a whole.

The British historian Arnold J. Toynbee (1889–1975) sounded a warning on this subject during our dialogue. He said that much of the misery in the world today stems from the fact that leaders in every area fail to seriously consider death, the fundamental issue of existence. This is a very wise observation. Far too many leaders avoid any self-reflection and focus solely on short-term interests.

If we avoid looking at death, any happiness that we achieve will be a fleeting illusion. It is by gaining a proper understanding of death that we really know how to live and how to contribute meaningfully to society and civilization.

Joy in Life, Joy in Death

NISHIYAMA: That is so true. What I felt most keenly when I faced the deaths of those three patients was the stark fact that our entire life is distilled in our last moments. Some die as peacefully as an old tree returning to the earth, while others experience pain and agony. Some are dearly missed by others when they die, while some are not. Still others die alone and friendless, with no one to watch over them.

When I observed those three deaths, for the first time I asked myself about the real meaning of life, what was the best way to live as a human being, and what was the essential nature of existence. That experience is actually what led me to seek a philosophy of life and death and thus join the Soka Gakkai.

IKEDA: That's very praiseworthy. Buddhism deals with the issue of birth and death head-on and offers answers that are universally convincing, clear, and at the same time profound.

The Record of the Orally Transmitted Teaching talks about birth, aging, sickness, and death, "When, while in these four states of birth, aging, sickness, and death, we chant Nam-myoho-renge-kyo, we cause them to waft forth the fragrance of the four virtues [of eternity, happiness, true self, and purity]" (OTT, 90).

In other words, by having faith in and practicing Nichiren Buddhism, birth is transformed into joy, aging and sickness become springboards to a higher state of life, and death becomes a glorious departure to eternal happiness. Nichiren promises us that we will be able to achieve a wonderful life state that savors joy in both life and death in lifetime after lifetime.

NISHIYAMA: You spoke of this view of existence, President Ikeda, during your second address at Harvard University (in 1993), titled "Mahayana Buddhism and Twenty-First-Century Civilization."[12] It received a tremendous response from leading world thinkers.

The Spanish Flu and World War I

IKEDA: Thank you. Getting back to influenza, when was it first identified?

HIRASAWA: The ancient Greek physician Hippocrates actually described influenza in his writings.

One of the major outbreaks in recent history was the 1918 epidemic of the Spanish flu. As many as 600 million people around the world contracted it, and more than 20 million died.[13]

NARUMI: In Japan alone, some 390,000 died. The 1957 Asian flu and the 1968 Hong Kong flu were also major outbreaks.

IKEDA: The Spanish flu occurred during World War I, and it killed so many soldiers that it is said to have hastened the end of the war.

How are those especially virulent outbreaks different from the flu that occurs annually?

HIRASAWA: The influenza virus evolves over time, so each year it causes a new outbreak. In most cases, however, it never attains the virulence of the Spanish flu.

NARUMI: There have also been cases when a completely new type of flu virus suddenly appears about ten years after a previous outbreak.

IKEDA: It's those new strains that cause the global flu epidemics, isn't it?

NARUMI: Yes. Because people don't have any resistance to the new virus, many succumb to it, as in the cases of the Spanish flu, the Asian flu, and the Hong Kong flu.

WHY NEW VIRUSES?

IKEDA: Recently, there has been the astonishing news that the Spanish flu actually derived from an avian influenza.

HIRASAWA: That's right. Waterfowl and other birds are frequently infected with the flu, but in most cases it cannot be passed to people. But when pigs are simultaneously infected with bird and human flu viruses, the viruses can mutate and give birth to a new virus that can infect people.

NARUMI: The concern right now is that close contact between people and birds may enable the bird flu virus to directly infect human beings, where it will mutate into a new virus that can be passed from person to person.

IKEDA: And with our highly developed transportation networks, it is feared that any new human flu virus will quickly spread around the world. Considering the contagiousness of the influenza virus, we mustn't take this matter lightly.

NISHIYAMA: Some predict that half of the world's population could be infected and many would die. Each of us faces the possibility of becoming the person who starts a global pandemic.

Always Take Precautions

HIRASAWA: The most dangerous enemy is carelessness. When the Spanish flu first erupted in 1918, the initial outbreak was from April through June. This preliminary influenza bout did not claim many victims in the United States, leading many to conclude that it wasn't a very serious illness and was only dangerous for the elderly. The government shared this opinion and took few precautions.

But in October that year, the number of cases and fatalities skyrocketed. More than 20 million U.S. citizens were infected and some 675,000 died. Moreover, perhaps because the virus had mutated in the intervening months, during this second outbreak many of the victims were young. By the time the government realized the seriousness of the situation, it was too late, and none of its countermeasures were effective.

IKEDA: In far too many instances, accidents arise out of the arrogance or carelessness of thinking somehow we'll be okay and that misfortune only befalls others. That's why it's important to always be alert and be firmly resolved to take precautions against illness or injury.

Careful Preparation Is the Key to Victory

NARUMI: During the time of the Spanish flu epidemic, there was apparently a town in the United States that, despite being located in an area infected by the virus, managed to escape a major outbreak.

IKEDA: That's an important fact. What happened?

NARUMI: Learning of the flu outbreak in the surrounding area, the town schoolteacher took prompt action. He employed all his knowledge and persistently advocated to the residents methods for treating and preventing the spread of the disease. Ultimately, he came up with a unique quarantine system for the town. As a result of these valiant efforts, the epidemic was kept at bay some eighteen miles outside the town's borders.

IKEDA: It was a victory derived from the teacher's unyielding determination and strong sense of responsibility to protect the town and the children. One person of solid commitment is stronger than ten thousand. The important thing is to have a constant sense of how to respond in a crisis and to prepare thoroughly in advance. If we casually presume that somehow things will work out, we're already doomed.

Such precautions as gargling and washing one's hands may seem like little things, but it's just those little things that are important. It's a mistake to minimize or overlook them. They can be the first step in preventing a widespread outbreak, and as such, they need to be taken seriously.

NISHIYAMA: Talking about this reminds me of the Hong Kong Soka Kindergarten. At the height of the fears surrounding the SARS (Severe Acute Respiratory Syndrome) epidemic in 2003, the kindergarten was recognized by the Hong Kong government for its model sanitation education.

IKEDA: That's right. Teachers used a quiz format to teach sound health practices like hand washing and gargling to the students. In addition to keeping the school spotlessly clean, every other precaution was taken to prevent infection and its spread.

HIRASAWA: When Professor Arthur Kwok Cheung Li, Hong Kong Education and Manpower secretary, visited the school, he remarked that it was indeed a perfect example of the educational ideal of making the growth of the children the top priority.

IKEDA: As the school's founder, I was delighted by this, and deeply grateful to the teaching staff.

NARUMI: A few years ago (in 2000), Professor Li, as vice chancellor of the Chinese University of Hong Kong, presented you with an honorary degree of doctor of social science.

IKEDA: I will never forget the vice chancellor's kindness as well as the solemn ceremony that was held on that occasion.

So what should you do if you catch the flu? I suppose rest is very important.

NISHIYAMA: That's correct. You need to drink plenty of fluids, eat nourishing foods, and rest. There is also medicine that can control the virus to a certain extent, and its appropriate use can alleviate the symptoms.

HIRASAWA: Another important thing is to avoid infecting others in your environment. If you have the flu, you should stay home from work and meetings.

NARUMI: That's right. Even when you start feeling a little better, you should continue to avoid attending meetings for a while, because the virus is still just as contagious. We strongly recommend that you stay in bed for two or three days after your fever has gone down.

Sympathy Is the Foundation for a Healthy Society

IKEDA: I hope everyone will observe this as the proper consideration we should show others. Earlier I noted that Shakyamuni had encouraged his disciples to take certain sanitary precautions such as washing their hands and gargling. At the time, Shakyamuni lived in a communal situation with his disciples. The illness of a single individual could easily have spread to the entire group. No doubt that concern was partially behind Shakyamuni's focus on hygiene.

In many cases, people are highly sensitive to their own sufferings while being oblivious to those of others. But influenza has the potential to become a global threat. Unless we take responsibility to protect not only ourselves but our families, neighbors, and friends, we can contribute to a tragedy of universal proportions. I am by no means exaggerating. A spiritual transformation in each individual—in other words, an elevation of their life state—is the most important preventative measure.

Nichiren says, "The varied sufferings that all living beings undergo—all these are Nichiren's own sufferings" (OTT, 138). The Buddhist spirit of sympathy, of placing yourself in another person's shoes, is the foundation for creating a century of health and life. It is the spirit most needed by humanity today.

4: Are Our Lives Determined by Our Genes?

IKEDA: Mr. Toda often said: "When you tally up all the joys and sufferings at the end of your life and subtract one from the other, what do you get? If there is more joy than suffering, then you are happy. If there's more suffering than joy, then you are unhappy." Mr. Toda, a mathematical genius, had a real knack for expressing things in this way.

Birth, aging, sickness, and death are the fundamental sufferings of life. In that sense, how we handle these facts of existence determines whether our life is happy or unhappy. Buddhism is a storehouse of wisdom for overcoming these four sufferings.

I'm certain that your actual experiences as dedicated doctors, conveyed vividly in your own words, will find deep resonance with our readers.

Hospitalization of Family Members

IKEDA: To continue in this spirit of openness, let me ask you, Dr. Hirasawa, if you've ever been hospitalized.

HIRASAWA: Yes, in the summer of 1998, I was in a traffic accident and suffered an injury to my cervical vertebrae, a broken wrist, and severe bruising all over my body. I was hospitalized for eight days. This happened just as I was making preparations to open a medical practice in Tokyo. I had a cast on one arm and a brace on the other. I was in terrible pain and couldn't turn over in bed; even pressing the button to call a nurse was difficult. My back was always soaked with sweat. What's more, the intravenous drips I was given every morning and evening were quite painful.

I even found it hard to explain my symptoms to my own doctor! Through that experience, I got a real taste of the pain and frustrations that patients endure.

IKEDA: Such an experience is bound to deepen a physician's compassion for his or her patients. And having family members hospitalized also causes one to reflect on one's life.

HIRASAWA: Yes. In May of 2002, my mother had a stroke. Her doctor said that there was little hope that an operation would save her life. I immediately received encouragement from you, President Ikeda, which helped me a great deal.

My mother raised six children while struggling against poverty. We all wished to do whatever we could for her, even if she would never regain her full faculties. I asked her doctor what he would do if it were his own mother, and after thinking about it for a while he replied that he'd arrange for her to have the surgery.

Fortunately, the surgery was a success. Through her experience, I have come to realize just how much trust and hope patients and their families place in their doctors.

IKEDA: Your mother imparted a golden lesson to you.

I once asked Dr. Felix Unger, a renowned Austrian cardiologist and president of the European Academy of Sciences and Arts, what he thought were the qualifications of a truly good physician. He said a good physician is someone who is completely dedicated to his or her patients, who works for and protects them day and night. Dr. Unger's words express an unwavering philosophy and conviction.

NISHIYAMA: We should all strive to be that way.

A Measure of Intelligence

IKEDA: A member of the young mothers group has asked us to discuss genetics. Do you mind if we talk about this?

NARUMI: Not at all. It's a topic of great interest to many.

IKEDA: Speaking of the deceased father of his young disciple Nanjo Tokimitsu, Nichiren Daishonin writes: "Now I wonder if he did not make himself young again and stay behind in the form of his precious, beloved son. Words fail me when I see that not only is there a perfect resemblance, but even his heart is the same" (WND-2, 495). There are certainly cases where children are so similar to their parents, it's uncanny. Is physical resemblance—like facial features and body type—primarily a matter of genetics?

NARUMI: Genetic inheritance definitely plays a major role. We know that such things as blood type and hair and eye color are genetically determined.

IKEDA: So what determines whether or not we are smart?

NISHIYAMA: Well, actually, it's a combination of individual effort, the environment, and genetics. I believe all of these factors play a part.

HIRASAWA: Research on the IQs of parents and children indicates that in general, children have a tendency to possess an IQ that is the average of both parents.

NARUMI: Of course, there are exceptions, and IQ is a measure of only one aspect of mental ability.

IKEDA: That's quite true. Though this isn't related to genetics, Mr. Toda used to say that a disciple who really listened to his mentor's teachings would become smarter.

Genetics and Personality

IKEDA: How about personality?

NISHIYAMA: There's some interesting research on that subject from the United States—a long-term study of identical twins raised separately.

IKEDA: Identical twins share the same genetic information, right?

NISHIYAMA: That's correct. This study looked into what happened to identical twins as a result of being brought up in different environments.

IKEDA: What did they find out?

NISHIYAMA: Even though the twins were raised in different environments and only met for the first time after age thirty, some sets of twins had nearly the same interests and personalities, even including the same taste in clothing. Some twins even ended up naming their children the same names. Several such cases were reported.

IKEDA: That's astonishing. That means that the influence of genetics is remarkably strong.

NISHIYAMA: The study suggested that two-thirds of our personality is genetically determined.

NARUMI: Two-thirds seems like a lot, but I think it's important to look at this from the other side: the fact that one-third of our personality is created by factors other than genetic inheritance is very significant. In other words, how we are raised and educated shape one-third of our personality, meaning that we have a very rich potential compared to other species. It demonstrates just how much human beings can be influenced by their education and socialization.

IKEDA: That's a very interesting perspective. The point, at any rate, is that personality and character are complex and multilayered rather than defined by either genetics or the environment.

HIRASAWA: That's right. Although, it would be very convenient if personality was completely determined by genetics—then we could blame all our bad points on our parents!

IKEDA: In essence, we each have to build our own future. A Buddhist scripture states: "If you want to understand the causes that existed in the past, look at the results as they are manifested in the present. And if you want to understand what results will be manifested in the future, look at the causes that exist in the present"[14] (WND-1, 279). Both our genetic makeup and our environment are the reality we must deal with, and at the same time they constitute the results of our past causes. What's crucial, however, is how we develop ourselves and how we transform our circumstances now toward the future. And Buddhism is what provides us the power to do just that.

The ancient Roman statesman Appius Claudius Caecus (340–273 BCE) wrote, "Every man is the architect of his own fortune." Taking control of our own fate and enabling our spirit to soar freely—this proactive attitude is what we call in Buddhism the spirit of true cause—the spirit of ever moving forward from this moment on. Making each present moment our point of departure and consistently striving to create a new self and a new world, we can realize a life brimming with ever greater vitality and hope. Therein lies the source of perpetual youth.

What Is a Genome?

IKEDA: Recently, there are frequent references to genome research in the media. What precisely is a genome?

HIRASAWA: A genome is the complete set of genetic information that is transmitted from parents to child through the union of sperm and egg. The word is a combination of *gene* and *chromosome*. Children thus inherit their genomes from their parents.

IKEDA: Genes are the information encoded within the genome, then?

NARUMI: That's right. Genes carry instructions for building proteins and other molecules that form the bodies of living things. According to 2001 research, there are some thirty thousand genes in the human genome.[15]

NISHIYAMA: This number surprised researchers, who had predicted that the human genome would consist of closer to one hundred thousand genes. The genome of the tiny fruit fly *Drosophila* has about thirty thousand genes, and even the common weed thale cress (*Arabidopsis thaliana*, the first plant to have its entire genome deciphered) has some twenty-six thousand genes.

IKEDA: In other words, on the genetic level, human beings aren't much different from other living things.

Genetic Indicators of Disease

IKEDA: Genetic research is rapidly advancing. How much will genetics be able to tell us about the individual?

HIRASAWA: Genetic research is helping us understand disease better. For example, we have identified the genes that cause hereditary disorders such as Huntington's Disease and neurofibromatosis. These diseases occur in individuals who carry a certain mutant gene.

NARUMI: While genetic testing can predict hereditary disorders, there is no guarantee that a cure exists for those disorders. Such testing should be conducted with utmost care.

IKEDA: Nichiren actually speaks of genetic diseases in his writings, saying, "Concerning the disease that is passed on to one's children, though it may be rare for children to resemble their parents in every particular, this kind of disease will most certainly be passed on to them" (WND-2, 497).

NISHIYAMA: That's amazing. This is an accurate description of genetic diseases.

NARUMI: Every individual carries six or seven genes that can cause diseases, even if the diseases don't manifest themselves. But most lifestyle diseases—for example, cancer, high blood pressure, and diabetes—stem from the interaction of various genes and environmental factors that determines whether the disease manifests. It is therefore difficult to predict whether an individual will contract any given disease in the future.

IKEDA: That's reasonable. The current research on genetics alone cannot tell us everything there is to know about the human condition—and, of course, it cannot determine whether a person enjoys a happy life or not.

I have met and talked with Dr. Sarvagya Singh Katiyar of India, a leading biochemist. He clearly told me that a person's genetic makeup cannot reveal anything about the kind of life he or she will lead.

NISHIYAMA: Yes, happiness is determined by the state of our hearts and minds.

Advice for Visiting Patients

IKEDA: Moving on to another subject, let me share another question from a reader. This person asks if we have any advice about how to behave when visiting people in the hospital.

NARUMI: At most hospitals, examinations and doctors' rounds take place in the morning, so from 2:00 to 5:00 p.m. is probably a good time to visit patients.

NISHIYAMA: It's also best to make your visit brief and not to overwhelm the patient with too many visitors at once. Avoid visiting right after the patient is hospitalized or immediately after surgery, and try not to bring children with you.

IKEDA: Do you have any other advice to offer?

NARUMI: It's not a good idea to repeat what you've heard about the patient's condition from his or her family members directly to the patient. In other words, respect the patient's privacy.

HIRASAWA: It's also very rude for visitors to whisper in front of patients. That only makes them worry that something is being kept from them.

NISHIYAMA: Another point is that when people are sick or undergoing certain treatments, they may be especially susceptible to nausea, so it might sometimes be best to refrain from wearing strong-smelling perfumes or hair creams, or bringing them highly fragrant flowers.

IKEDA: Florence Nightingale advised nurses to minimize "the expense of vital power by the patient"[16]—that is, not to sap their vitality. When visiting the sick, one of the most important guidelines is not to tire them. There are times when visiting can actually be a burden for the patient. We need to be considerate and act wisely. Patients can be quite sensitive.

HIRASAWA: That's so true. For example, sometimes constantly urging the patient to get well and to keep on fighting can do more harm than good. After all, no one is more concerned about making a quick recovery than patients themselves.

NISHIYAMA: Sincerely wishing someone well can be encouraging, but a thoughtless "Get better!" can actually be a source of pressure for the patient.

IKEDA: That's a significant point. We should take care not to pressure or cause stress to patients. The most important thing is to put their minds at ease.

NARUMI: That's right. People who tend to suffer in silence not wanting to worry others may not be forthcoming about any pain or anxieties they may have. Lending them a sympathetic ear can therefore be the best encouragement.

IKEDA: Yes, making patients feel that they are supported and understood is probably the most important thing. Moreover, the words of solace that just naturally come to us are likely to be the most effective in comforting them.

The Remarkable Power of Encouragement

NISHIYAMA: To give patients peace of mind, it's also important to take concrete measures to alleviate their concerns. When treatment continues for an extended period, people worry about missing work or school. Mothers worry about family finances and about not being able to run their households or care for their children.

IKEDA: In a letter, Nichiren Daishonin reassures an ailing disciple, Myoichi, saying: "I may yet gain influence in this lifetime. If so, rest assured that I will look after your children" (WND-1, 536). Myoichi was caring for her two children, one of whom was very sick, in spite of the fact that she had lost her husband and was also in poor health herself. No doubt these sincere words from Nichiren were a tremendous source of encouragement and hope for her.

NARUMI: A kind word can make all the difference. Patients who have had a stroke and lost mobility in parts of their body often become discouraged by the slow process of their physical recovery and are quick to throw in the towel. But warm reassurance that they will eventually improve and wholehearted support from their caregivers usually provide them with the hope they need to keep working at their physical therapy.

HIRASAWA: Feeling reassured is very important. The confidence that stroke patients gain from being told that they will definitely get better is believed to stimulate their brains and hasten their recovery.

IKEDA: This is a prime example of the "oneness of body and mind." Just a few words of sincere encouragement can have a very powerful effect on a sick person. In a letter of encouragement to Toki Jonin when his wife was ill, Nichiren writes, "I am as concerned about the illness of your wife, the lay nun Toki, as though it were I myself who is ailing, and day and night I pray to the heavenly gods that she will recover" (WND-2, 666). The infinite compassion of the Daishonin is apparent in that simple phrase—"as though it were I myself who is ailing."

HIRASAWA: Sharing the problems and sufferings of others as if they were our own is the essence of Buddhist compassion and the Soka Gakkai spirit.

TREATING PATIENTS' FAMILIES

NISHIYAMA: Patients' families are also subject to a lot of stress.

IKEDA: Yes, the family not only has to care for the person who is ill but deal with financial and other practical matters. And the effort to protect the patient from such worries often causes them further stress.

NARUMI: Research shows that cancer patients and their families equally suffer from depression. As a result, it's recommended to treat the families as a sort of second patient.

HIRASAWA: It's very important to express appreciation and sympathy for the family's efforts.

IKEDA: Toki Jonin's wife cared assiduously for her mother-in-law, who was over ninety years old. Keenly aware of this, Nichiren praised her sincerely:

> Toki has told me that, while grieved at his mother's death, he was grateful that she passed away peacefully, and that you gave her such attentive care. He said joyfully that he would never be able to forget this in any lifetime to come. (WND-1, 656)

Mothers and wives often bear the heaviest burden in nursing and caring for the ill. It's important to recognize their tireless efforts and offer them encouragement and moral support.

THE DANGERS OF GENETIC TESTING

IKEDA: To return to the subject of genetics, Dr. Unger issued an important warning, noting that though our present understanding of genes remains incomplete, genetic data could be used to refuse medical insurance to people with genetic markers for diseases that they might contract at some future point or to deny people employment. Instead of empowering and assisting people, he said, such genetic testing could end up as a threat to health and well-being.

NISHIYAMA: Advances in genetics raise many complex issues, privacy among them. The use of genetic testing to deny people insurance or to discriminate in employment would be a terrible perversion of medical science.

NARUMI: Mistaken beliefs about genetics have often been used to support prejudice and discrimination in the past. The Nazi-era eugenics movement, for example, claimed that different ethnic groups could be ranked as genetically superior or inferior, and this theory was used to support the mass murder of Jews in the Holocaust.

IKEDA: And this way of thinking is not a thing of the past. Certain people today still stubbornly subscribe to the fallacious notion that genes determine a person's superiority or inferiority.

HIRASAWA: In 1994, a book was published in the United States arguing that intelligence is hereditary, and that children of certain ethnic groups are therefore genetically destined to be intellectually inferior. As a result, the book asserted, educational support for them should be cut. It sold more than half a million copies.

IKEDA: That is truly lamentable. Nothing is more frightening than when science is misused with ill intent or prejudice or spreads misinformation.

NARUMI: The fact that the book was written by well-known university professors amplified its influence. The renowned biologist and Harvard professor Stephen J. Gould (1941–2002) criticized it, saying that the authors "violate fairness by converting a complex case ... into a biased brief for permanent and heritable difference."[17]

IKEDA: I've met Dr. Gould. We both received honorary doctorates from the University of Glasgow during the same ceremony (in June 1994). It was a very solemn occasion. Dr. Gould stressed that intelligence is not some static, unchanging quality determined by such factors as genetics or race. Rather, he insisted, it is highly responsive to the environment.

HIRASAWA: That's absolutely true.

ALL LIFE IS SACRED

IKEDA: Science should contribute to the happiness and welfare of humanity. It should protect the dignity of life. The time has come for scientists to reaffirm this fundamental purpose.

The eminent plant geneticist Dr. M. S. Swaminathan, president of the Pugwash Conferences on Science and World Affairs, asserted that modern genetic research indicates that almost all living organisms share a common genetic code. This implies, he said, that all life forms are sacred. A Buddhist scripture states, "A plant, a tree, a pebble, a speck of dust—each has the Buddha nature"[18] (WND-1, 356).

NISHIYAMA: Buddhism teaches that our lives are supremely noble and encompass the entire universe.

IKEDA: Contemporary humanity has a great deal of information and technology at its command, but it seems to have lost sight of the all-embracing wisdom of this holistic view of life, humanity, nature, and the universe. The twenty-first century is the century of the life sciences, and the exploration of life is certain to deepen and advance. There is thus a need for a wisdom and philosophy that enable us to use our knowledge and technology for the happiness of humanity.

Our proud mission as people who uphold and practice Nichiren Buddhism is to respond to the needs of our time and make this a century of respect for the sanctity of life.

5: Children and Stress

Narumi: We are joined now by Dr. Boey Chiong Meng, head of the Soka Gakkai Malaysia doctors division.

Dr. Boey Chiong Meng: President Ikeda, thank you for inviting me to participate!

Ikeda: It's been a long time! I'm glad to see you looking so well.

Boey: During your trip to Malaysia in 2000, I was able to establish a wonderful new starting point for my life. I wish to thank you most sincerely for that opportunity.

Nishiyama: Your Japanese is excellent, Dr. Boey.

Boey: I have been studying hard in hopes of being able to speak directly to President Ikeda someday. My wife, who studied at Soka University in Japan, also helped me.

Ikeda: Soka Gakkai Malaysia has developed dynamically. The social contributions made by your organization have gained trust and praise from all sectors of Malaysian society.

Boey: Thank you for your kind words. When you visited, the Malaysia doctors division was a newly established group with eighteen members. Now we are more than thirty strong.

IKEDA: That's wonderful. SGI members around the world are shining brilliantly as model citizens of their communities.

Inheriting a Father's Dream

IKEDA: Why did you decide to become a physician, Dr. Boey?

BOEY: It was my father's influence. The death of his younger sister at a young age had made him want to become a doctor, but he was forced to give up his dream due to financial reasons.

NISHIYAMA: You inherited your father's dream, then.

BOEY: That's right. When I was seventeen, I enrolled in a high school in the United Kingdom. I studied hard and chanted a lot, and I decided that I wanted to become a doctor. I was eventually accepted to the University of London Medical School.

IKEDA: Once we awaken to our mission, our inherent abilities blossom quickly.

Dr. Boey, you followed your chosen path unswervingly and became a qualified physician. Now you are an assistant professor in the medical department of the University of Malaya, right?

BOEY: Yes. I'm also working as a pediatrician at the university hospital.

The Declining Number of Pediatricians

IKEDA: Are there many pediatricians in Malaysia?

BOEY: Yes. Because children form a large percentage of our population, we have a relatively high number of pediatricians.

NARUMI: In Japan, despite a general rise in the number of physicians, the number of pediatricians is decreasing.[19]

NISHIYAMA: Because pediatrics is a very challenging yet relatively low-paying field of medicine, many medical students are staying away from it.

IKEDA: That's a matter for deep concern. Japan's overall medical system needs to be improved. Children are the precious treasures of the future. They are earth's greatest natural resource. Protecting their invaluable lives is protecting the future of humanity. No mission is more noble or important than this.

President Toda always emphasized the need for society as a whole to value elementary school teachers. The same should apply to pediatricians.

Ten Percent of Children Have Psychosomatic Disorders

IKEDA: What kind of research have you been involved in, Dr. Boey?

BOEY: A recent survey of some three thousand elementary school students in Malaysia revealed that about 10 percent of them suffered from stomachaches intense enough to interfere with their daily lives. In most cases, this was identified as stress-induced psychosomatic illness. I earned my degree researching this subject.

NISHIYAMA: Studies show that psychosomatic disorders are rising annually among Japanese children too. Reports from the United Kingdom, Canada, and the United States also suggest that 10 percent of children in those countries suffer from such disorders.

IKEDA: What causes stress in children?

BOEY: Numerous causes have been identified, among them the illness or death of a close relative or loved one, a parent's unemployment, family discord, abuse, and pressures at school, such as exams or bullying.

NISHIYAMA: I think that physical factors such as poor nutrition and lack of sleep can also play a significant role.

IKEDA: Child abuse and bullying mustn't be tolerated. And when children face illness or death in their families, they need appropriate support and care.
How does stress lead to chronic illness?

Paying Attention to Warning Signs

BOEY: Symptoms such as stomachaches are a child's cry for help. Parents may not realize this, or if they do, their efforts to alleviate the problem can end up putting further pressure on the child and exacerbating the situation. This can lead to chronic illness.

NARUMI: There is a Japanese saying about children being oblivious to their parents' feelings, but in this case parents are often oblivious to their children's true feelings. To avoid this, parents need to make an effort each day to recognize the warning signs in their children.

IKEDA: The Buddhist scriptures also compare the compassion of the Buddha to that of parents who, though they love all their children equally, are especially attentive to those who are ill.

If parents make an effort to communicate sincerely and openly with their children at all times, they will notice even the most subtle changes in their moods and behavior.

The Importance of Listening

NISHIYAMA: It worries me to see so many mothers who come to the hospital where I work rushing their children and telling them to hurry up. I imagine that when their children come home from school and want to talk to them about something, those mothers are probably telling them: "Hurry up and change your clothes!" "Hurry up and do your homework!"

IKEDA: How do you greet the children who come to your hospital, Dr. Boey?

BOEY: When children come to my examination room they are anxious and nervous, so I always start by listening to what they have to say.

IKEDA: Listening is very important, isn't it?

BOEY: It is. In order to ease their minds and make them feel comfortable and relaxed, I spend from forty-five minutes to an hour gently asking them detailed questions and trying to earn their trust.

NARUMI: The current state of Japanese hospitals makes it very difficult for doctors to have lengthy consultations with patients. Even so, doctors should refrain from firing a barrage of questions at their patients and rushing through the examination. This applies to adults as well as children.

IKEDA: It's certainly true that when the doctor is in a hurry, the patient feels pressured and tense.

NISHIYAMA: That's right. And parents also need to be careful that, when their child comes to them with an ailment, they avoid using words and actions that cause the child to have feelings of doubt, despair, or alienation.

IKEDA: Children are very sensitive. They understand much more than adults imagine. That's why it's crucial to trust and respect children as individuals in their own right, never being condescending toward them. I have always tried to approach children as equals.

BOEY: Adults need to keep in mind that abusive words or attitudes are a kind of emotional violence that can inflict deep scars.

Bolstering Self-confidence Promotes Growth

IKEDA: Children must be encouraged to freely realize their potential. They should be praised when they strive to achieve something. No matter how small it is, we should commend them, even going a little over the top to do so. Giving children the confidence that they can do something if they try is a tremendous source of growth. Making them feel inferior, on the other hand, only stunts their potential.

NISHIYAMA: The smallest things can determine whether a child loses hope or grows by leaps and bounds.

IKEDA: It comes down to parents' attitudes—whether or not they believe in their child's potential.

This year (2005), my dialogue with Dr. Ved Nanda, an authority on international law at the University of Denver in the United States, was published in Japanese.[20] Dr. Nanda's memories of his mother made a deep impression on me. "My mother never spoke ill of family members or friends," he said. "All her life she always tried to see what was good in everyone and to praise it."[21]

NISHIYAMA: What a wonderful mother!

IKEDA: I'm sure she also equally showered Dr. Nanda and her other children with utmost praise when they were growing up. All people are worthy of the highest respect and have infinite potential. Carrying on this spiritual legacy of his mother, Dr. Nanda has become a global champion of human rights and justice.

"Retired Husband Syndrome"

IKEDA: Speaking of stress, Dr. Boey, something called "retired husband syndrome" has become a focus of attention in Japan lately.

BOEY: This is the first time I've heard of it.

NISHIYAMA: It's a syndrome seen in housewives who are stressed out by suddenly having their retired husbands at home all the time.

BOEY: What kind of symptoms does it present?

NARUMI: High blood pressure, ulcers, bronchial asthma, and depression.

NISHIYAMA: According to Nobuo Kurokawa's *Shin shujin zaitaku sutoresu shokogun* (The New Retired Husband Syndrome), a combination of psychosomatic and psychiatric therapy is called for. At the same time, the couple must make a concerted effort to deal with the problem.

Kurokawa suggests that the husband has to recognize that he's the cause of his wife's stress and avoid being domineering or demanding. The wife also needs to learn to be more assertive and to clearly express her feelings and needs.

IKEDA: No doubt they should both make an effort before they reach retirement age to be considerate of and to express their appreciation to one another.

NARUMI: Instead of staying cooped up at home all the time, they should probably go out and find some activity they can do together or find some way they can contribute to their community. Those are good ways to relieve stress. When we feel that we have some purpose and that we are making a difference, our life force is stimulated and strengthened.

IKEDA: Soka Gakkai activities incorporate many of these elements. Moreover, it is by joyously striving for the well-being of others and society that we build a golden foundation of happiness in our lives. How fortunate we are! There is no healthier way to live.

I hope that our men's division members, in particular, will do their utmost to participate vigorously in Soka Gakkai activities—for the sake of their wives and to promote their own health.

Preventing Malpractice

IKEDA: Recently, medical malpractice has become a hot topic in Japan. What's the situation in other countries?

BOEY: There are cases of medical malpractice in Malaysia as well. When a patient is harmed or dies, the case often ends up in the courts.

NARUMI: I've heard that the same is true in the United Kingdom and Germany. Influenced by the United States, where such civil suits are relatively common, malpractice suits seem to be increasing in many nations.

IKEDA: Patients' lives depend upon the medical treatment they receive. It is therefore crucial that every effort be made to prevent medical errors or malpractice.

With a view to preventing medical errors, Dr. Unger stressed the importance of thoroughly investigating the situations in which errors have occurred and why.

NISHIYAMA: I completely agree. The Japanese Ministry of Health, Labor, and Welfare has begun creating a near-miss database. It is important for doctors to learn from these cases and heighten their awareness of potential medical errors. There is a need to put in place thorough cross-checking procedures to prevent such errors.

IKEDA: Dr. Unger also noted the bureaucracy of hospitals as an additional problem. At his own hospital, he is adamant about avoiding becoming bureaucratic, saying ironically that bureaucracy functions effectively only when there are no patients.

Genuine medical reform begins from the idea that doctors cannot exist without patients.

True Fulfillment in Life

IKEDA: Dr. Boey, have you had any unforgettable patients?

BOEY: Yes. I especially remember a young woman who was a member of the Malaysia junior high school division who had a case of acute leukemia.

NISHIYAMA: That's a very serious illness.

BOEY: She was hospitalized in December 2003. From the beginning, she was aware just how critical her condition was. In an effort to relieve her anxieties about death, she began to read President Ikeda's writings, and through them she learned that the degree of fulfillment one experiences in life is determined by how one has lived.

IKEDA: Nichiren writes, "It is better to live a single day with honor than to live to 120 and die in disgrace" (WND-1, 851). The sense of fulfillment we gain from knowing that we have really contributed to the well-being of others and society is imperishable. It is engraved in our lives as eternal good fortune and benefit.

BOEY: As a matter of fact, when I was a child, I used to have the same worry as my patient—"What happens to us after we die?" That was what led me to join the Soka Gakkai. Through striving in faith, practice, and study, I have attained a personal understanding of the profound Buddhist principle of the eternity of life.

IKEDA: No doubt having you as her doctor was a great source of encouragement for her.

Keep On Going

BOEY: Thank you. While she was hospitalized, she underwent intensive chemotherapy and radiation treatments and, after several months, she recovered. In 2004, in spite of her long absence from school, she sat for the national examinations and received top marks.

NISHIYAMA: What a wonderful story of recovery!

BOEY: But her illness returned in January of this year (2005). Nevertheless, her fighting spirit burned ever brighter. The entire hospital staff was deeply moved by her positive, cheerful attitude.

NARUMI: Generally, when people contract a serious illness, they often complain about the pain and their life force weakens. People with strong faith in Nichiren Buddhism, however, use sickness as an opportunity to galvanize their life force.

BOEY: In Malaysia, we have a proverb: "If your cane breaks, use your hands and knees." It means that it's pointless to just passively lament misfortune. We have to keep on going. When we're struggling with illness, we need to have a firm determination not to let it defeat us.

IKEDA: That's very true. When the youthful Nanjo Tokimitsu was very ill, the Daishonin repudiated the devils of illness and death with tremendous force:

> You demons, by making this man suffer, are you trying to swallow a sword point first, or embrace a raging fire, or become the archenemy of the Buddhas of the ten directions in the three existences? How terrible this will be for you! Should you not cure this man's illness immediately, act rather as his protectors, and escape from the grievous sufferings that are the lot of demons? (WND-1, 1109)

Thanks to Nichiren's prayers and guidance, Tokimitsu lived another fifty years, during which he strove energetically for kosen-rufu.

Taking the Daishonin's words deeply to heart, I, too, pray earnestly for the recovery and long life of all our members fighting illness, as well as for the health and happiness of their families.

Doctors Must Never Give Up

Boey: My patient once shared her dream with me, saying, "I want to study at Soka University, the school President Ikeda founded." Her condition was declining with each passing day. In an effort to encourage her, I shared with her a poem that you had dedicated to the Soka schools students:

> *Nothing in this world*
> *is more important*
> *than mentor and disciple.*
> *Never forget, my friends*
> *these ties of victory.*

I'll never forget the smile on her face on that occasion. And she never lost her smile, up to the moment she peacefully passed away in March of this year (2005). I learned so much from her example. Life is constantly changing, moment by moment. Encouragement inspires hope and the will to live. Most doctors know this, but in many cases they give up. That's why it's so important for doctors who practice Nichiren Buddhism to compassionately share their patients' suffering and encourage them warmly to the very end.

I am convinced that she triumphed over illness.

IKEDA: Nichiren praises the lay priest Ishikawa no Hyoe's daughter (Nanjo Tokimitsu's niece), who died from an illness at an early age. Noting how she had remained steadfast in her faith to the very end, he lauds her, saying, "How admirable, how worthy!" (WND-1, 903). He also observes that among his disciples, it is those who think themselves well versed in Buddhism who make errors, and he hails this young woman as a model for all to emulate.

BOEY: The Daishonin's spirit is very moving.

IKEDA: The lives of those who have dedicated themselves to upholding the Mystic Law shine with the life state of Buddhahood not only in this existence but after death as well. Encouraging Nanjo Tokimitsu's mother on the death of her husband, the Daishonin writes: "When he was alive, he was a Buddha in life, and now he is a Buddha in death. He is a Buddha in both life and death" (WND-1, 456).

Death is a phase of recharging in preparation for a new life. It's a kind of sleep. If you fall asleep as a Buddha, you will awaken in your new life as a Buddha. There is no sadness or misery on the eternal journey of those who passed away. Their life is filled with hope and so is their death. According to Nichiren's writings, they will be quickly reborn close to us, with a new life.

NISHIYAMA: The important thing is for the family members of the deceased to remain hopeful and continue pursuing their chosen path.

BOEY: Fortunately, the parents of my young patient felt assured that their daughter had won. At the same time, they were of course deeply saddened by the loss of their beloved child.

Joy in Both Life and Death

NISHIYAMA: The shock of losing a child is something that others cannot fully understand. The sense of loss feels like a huge abyss has opened in your heart.

IKEDA: That feeling of emptiness is not quickly relieved. It does indeed take time for the wound to heal. That period of grieving is very sorrowful and painful. The Daishonin sent the following encouragement to Nanjo Tokimitsu's mother when she lost her beloved son Shichiro Goro (Tokimitsu's younger brother):

> It was this splendid sutra that the late Shichiro Goro put his faith in and through which he attained Buddhahood. And today, on the forty-ninth day following his passing, all the Buddhas have surely gathered about him in the pure land of Eagle Peak, seating him on their palms, patting his head, embracing him, and rejoicing, welcoming him with affection as one would welcome a moon that has just risen, or blossoms that have just burst into bloom. (WND-1, 1075)

The life of her deceased child, Nichiren assures her, has fused with the Buddhahood of the universe, where it is embraced, protected, and cared for by all the Buddhas. Since he has achieved such a state of life, there is no reason to worry about him. This is truly what it means to savor joy in both life and death.

Since this is the case, the families of those who have passed away should continue leading their lives with strength, optimism, and courage. They should become happy no matter what. Living this way is proof of the attainment of Buddhahood of their deceased loved ones, and it sends waves of joy to them.

Those who have devoted their lives to kosen-rufu are certain to die a magnificent death, as peaceful as the setting sun slipping gloriously below the horizon.

The same can be applied to this year that is now almost past. Just as a beautiful sunset heralds a brilliant new day ahead, the lives of all of you who have striven together with the Soka Gakkai to achieve victory upon victory this year will shine again in the new year in good health, prosperity, and great victory. With such conviction, let's set forth in high spirits into the coming year!

6: A Constructive Approach to Aging

IKEDA: Though spring has officially started according to the old Japanese calendar, it's still quite cold outside.[22] I hope that our elderly members belonging to the Many Treasures Group will take care of their health, guarding against colds and also traffic accidents.

Morning and night, I pray earnestly for the well-being of our elderly members. They are all truly great individuals who have striven diligently over many long years for the sake of their friends, the Mystic Law, their communities, and society at large. They are the most precious treasures of the Soka Gakkai. I hope they will exercise wisdom as they go about their daily activities, being careful not to overdo it when they aren't feeling well or the weather outside is bad.

NARUMI: Out of the wish that our honored elderly members will live long, healthy lives, we will focus on the topic of aging in the next few chapters. Recently, terms such as "anti-aging" and "successful aging" have become buzzwords. This reflects that people are thinking more and more about how to remain healthy both physically and mentally as they age, and how to live to the end with optimism and a sense of purpose.

IKEDA: This is an important subject. Japan has one of the longest life expectancies in the world. But just because people are living longer doesn't necessarily mean that they are happy.

The ancient Roman philosopher Seneca (4 BCE–65 CE) said, "Let us cherish and love old age; for it is full of pleasure if one knows how to use it."[23] How can we put these words into action and make old age an enriching and fulfilling time of our lives? This is the fundamental challenge facing our graying society, and one that has become increasingly more pressing.

NARUMI: Dr. Makoto Michikawa of Japan's National Institute for Longevity Sciences (also Aichi doctors division vice leader) and Reiko Inamitsu, senior adviser of the women's division Shirakaba Group (nurses group), will join us from today to offer us their valuable insights on this subject.

MICHIKAWA AND INAMITSU: Thank you.

IKEDA: Thank you for your participation. Dr. Michikawa, what areas in particular are you researching with regard to longevity sciences?

DR. MAKOTO MICHIKAWA: One area of focus is the causes and trigger mechanisms of Alzheimer's disease, a leading cause of dementia and memory loss in the elderly. I'm also looking for safe and effective preventative measures and treatments.

IKEDA: This is essential research for an aging society. Ms. Inamitsu, you were a lecturer at Tokai University Junior College of Nursing and Technology in Kanagawa, right?

REIKO INAMITSU: Yes. When I was head nurse at Keio University Hospital, I was invited to assist with the establishment of Tokai University's nursing college. In 2003, I retired and am now (as of February 2006) an instructor in Soka University's Division of Correspondence Education.

IKEDA: I understand that you studied for your teaching credentials while working as a nurse. I hope you will share that valuable experience with others who are also studying while working full time.

INAMITSU: My students are all wonderful and I am determined to do my very best for them.

The Aging Process

IKEDA: Moving to the topic of our discussion today, what is the cause of the phenomenon we call aging?

MICHIKAWA: Some researchers believe that, based on the idea of built-in obsolescence, the aging process is switched on by an inner genetic clock. Others take the view that damage caused to DNA and proteins by reactive oxygen and other toxic substances over time manifests as what we call aging. The second theory carries more weight at present, but there is still much to uncover regarding the aging process.

IKEDA: How is reactive oxygen different from oxygen itself?

NARUMI: Oxygen is necessary in the process of breaking down at the cellular level the nutrients from the foods we eat and releasing energy. About 2 percent of that oxygen turns into reactive oxygen inside the body. Reactive oxygen is also generated through exposure to ultraviolet and other radiation.

Reactive oxygen is like a static electricity-charged ball, causing chemical reactions and changes in the substances that it comes into contact with.

Michikawa: It is believed that reactive oxygen causes damage to DNA and to the lipid and protein components of cell membranes, preventing cells from functioning properly and leading to such things as cancer and aging. Of course, the body also possesses the ability to neutralize this oxygen to a certain degree.

Reactive oxygen has positive effects, too, such as killing viruses and bacteria and helping eliminate toxins.

Ikeda: I see. At about what age does aging begin?

Narumi: Generally, adolescence marks the end of growth, and from about twenty-five on we begin to age.

Ikeda: Twenty-five! That seems very early!

Inamitsu: Of course, there are individual differences in the aging process.

Ikeda: A Buddhist scripture says that human life is a step-by-step journey to death. That's why it's so important to live each day of our youth and our entire life conscientiously and without regret.

Preventing Accidents Indoors

Ikeda: There are some obvious signs of aging we may experience as we get older, among them deteriorating eyesight or hearing, but what other kinds of evidence are there?

Michikawa: Difficulty walking or lifting heavy things, which suggest a decline in physical strength and endurance, as well as taking more time to recover from exertion are certainly clear indicators that we're getting old.

NARUMI: We all have a sense of our physical capabilities, and when for the first time we are unable to do something we always used to do, we are made aware that we're aging.

IKEDA: What about changes in senses other than sight and hearing?

NARUMI: Our sense of taste may change, leading to a preference for saltier foods. We also produce less saliva.

INAMITSU: Surprisingly, our sense of smell may also deteriorate. This can lead to older people not being able to smell a gas leak, resulting in household accidents. Elderly people living alone should have a gas-leak detector installed if possible.

IKEDA: That's good advice. Osteoporosis is also a sign of aging, isn't it?

NARUMI: That's right. As we age, our bones can become brittle and the muscles supporting them can weaken, so we may become more susceptible to broken bones. For the elderly, a broken bone can lead to becoming bedridden.

IKEDA: I've heard that more elderly people are killed by falls within the home than by traffic accidents. It's crucial to take every precaution to prevent slips and falls in the home.

INAMITSU: That's very true. One can trip on something as thin as the edge of a carpet, so it's important to be on guard at all times. One good preventative method is to keep the house orderly and tidy. Sudden changes in interior decor or remodeling should also be avoided. It takes elderly people longer to get used to a new environment, and unexpected changes can lead to accidents. Simple measures like not putting things on high shelves and immediately wiping up any spills on the floor can make a big difference.

Procrastination as a Sign of Aging

Ikeda: It's the little things that are important.

Inamitsu: Speaking of keeping one's home environment neat and orderly, President Ikeda, your friend, the actress Hideko Takamine, once wrote: "You start to age the first time you think, 'I have to clean that up,' and then say to yourself, 'Oh, why bother now? I can do it tomorrow. . . .'"

Ikeda: She certainly has a point!

I'm friends with both Ms. Takamine and her husband, the screenwriter Zenzo Matsuyama. I'll never forget how Mr. Matsuyama once praised the worldwide people's movement of the Soka Gakkai as "a mountain range of humanity."

Are there any other signs of aging we should mention?

Michikawa: As far as external signs, graying and loss of hair as well as skin wrinkling are the most obvious.

Narumi: Some physicians have called aging a process of drying out and hardening.

Ikeda: Youth is often described in such terms as "fresh" and "supple." Does that mean that as we age, we get dry and stiff?

Michikawa: Basically, yes. At birth, water accounts for about 80 percent of our body weight. In adulthood, that declines to 65 to 70 percent, and in the twilight years, it can decline to about two-thirds of what it was at birth. With the loss of water, our body's tissues "dry out." In addition, changes in collagen and the accumulation of waste materials cause tissues to lose elasticity.

INAMITSU: The skin starts to sag and gradually wrinkles form. At the same time, the body loses its flexibility and grows stiff. Both of these are conspicuous signs of aging.

Preserving Our Strength

IKEDA: As we get older, we may also have a reduced sense of thirst, right?

MICHIKAWA: Yes. It's therefore important to make a conscious effort to drink plenty of water. Instead of drinking a large amount all at once, though, it's better to drink small amounts regularly throughout the day.

INAMITSU: We should make a point of encouraging elderly people to drink plenty of water.

NARUMI: When we age, our kidneys may not function as well as they used to and we may require more water to eliminate bodily wastes. Some people don't drink water in the evenings because they wish to avoid nighttime trips to the bathroom, but this can be harmful, because it's easy to get dehydrated. In fact, drinking a sufficient amount of water is a good precaution for preventing strokes.

IKEDA: Buddhism teaches that our "veins [are] like the rivers and streams" (WND-2, 849). Our blood must flow throughout our bodies as freely and unobstructed as a river of pure, clean water flowing ceaselessly through the land. Toward that end, it is vital to drink lots of water.

Physically speaking, what are good ways to keep our bodies limber and flexible?

MICHIKAWA: Moderate exercise such as walking daily is helpful. Having said that, though, I wouldn't advise suddenly taking up some very strenuous sport or activity. The muscles, joints, bones, and the respiratory and circulatory systems can't adapt to sudden changes. It's better to take up an exercise regimen suited to your physical condition and stick with it.

IKEDA: That makes sense. So when we're young, we should focus on forging and strengthening our mind and body, and from forty on, we should concentrate more on preserving and maintaining that strength.

IMPORTANCE OF FOSTERING OTHERS

IKEDA: Though our bodies may get stiff as we age, it's crucial to keep our minds flexible and open! The older we get, the more we should listen to the opinions of others, especially those of young people, and the more we should encourage young people and help them surpass us in achievement.

NARUMI: Older people should warmly watch over the growth and development of the young.

IKEDA: The eminent educator Inazo Nitobe (1862–1933), an acquaintance of President Makiguchi, wrote, "What I wish to avoid is the infirmity of age—not the inevitable physical infirmity nor the mental, but those senile habits of finding fault with the young or of boasting of one's past career."[24] This is something that men in particular need to watch out for!

Incidentally, I recently saw a report on a very interesting study conducted in the United Kingdom. Using brain-imaging technology, University of London researchers examined whether men or women were more likely to delight in pain being inflicted on others.

MICHIKAWA: I was surprised to hear about this study too. Unfortunately, the conclusion was that this is more common among men!

IKEDA: That's right. Men showed no sympathetic response at all when someone they disliked was suffering.

The Spirit to Never Stop Growing

IKEDA: The elderly need to keep a spirit of challenge burning in their hearts for the sake of the next generation. Dr. Guy Bourgeault of the University of Montreal was a model of just such a forward-looking attitude.

He has said: "I consider it mistaken to associate openness and flexibility with youth and obtuse rigidity with old age.... It seemed easier for me to be open and to accept new things when I was forty and even fifty than it had been when I was twenty."[25]

I think that the true mark of youth is having the spiritual fortitude to never stop growing.

INAMITSU: I agree. Chronological age and old age are not necessarily the same thing.

IKEDA: That's true. If young people don't forge themselves spiritually, they won't shine with youthfulness. Only those whose spirits have been tested and strengthened through inner struggle based on the desire to achieve lofty goals will shine with the brilliance of youth.

Actively Carrying Out One's Mission

NARUMI: Many of the world leaders you've met with, President Ikeda, including Dr. Bourgeault, are still quite active and youthful in spirit. And all of them have remarked on your youthfulness and energy.

IKEDA: Thank you. As was mentioned earlier, drying up physically is a natural part of aging. Even so, we must be careful not to allow our hearts to dry up. As the French writer André Maurois (1885–1967) said: "Old age is far more than white hair, wrinkles, the feeling that it is too late and the game finished, that the stage belongs to the rising generations. The true evil is not the weakening of the body, but the indifference of the soul."[26] Regardless of their age, leading thinkers around the world remain vibrantly active on the stage of their mission.

NARUMI: I did a little checking, and that's certainly true in the case of many of the world leaders you've met with. British historian Arnold Toynbee was eighty-three when you first met; Austregésilo de Athayde (1898–1993) of the Brazilian Academy of Letters was ninety-four; the renowned chemist Linus Pauling was eighty-five, as were American business tycoon Armand Hammer (1898–1990) and Gandhi's disciple B. N. Pande (1906–98); and Joseph Rotblat (1908–2005), later president emeritus of the Pugwash Conferences, was eighty.

INAMITSU: The Chinese artist Fang Zhaoling (1914–2006) was eighty-two, and the American civil rights activist Rosa Parks

(1913–2005) received congratulations from you and Mrs. Ikeda on her eightieth birthday at the Calabasas campus of Soka University of America.

Dedication to a Lofty Goal Is the Source of a Youthful Spirit

Ikeda: Yes, that's right. In Dr. Pauling's case, he traveled some five hundred miles from San Francisco to visit the Calabasas campus, saying that he was happy to cooperate with us in any way he could for the sake of world peace. And Dr. Rotblat, who passed away last year (in 2005) at age ninety-six, said during our dialogue that he still had much to do to ensure that peace prevailed in the world.

As champions of peace and human rights age, they burn with ever greater passion to do more, to continue advancing for the sake of humanity and the future. To live dedicated to a lofty goal is the source of an eternally youthful spirit.

Michikawa: In that sense, the members of the Soka Gakkai's Many Treasures Group, people earnestly dedicated to the wonderful aim of kosen-rufu, are outstanding models of that spirit.

Ikeda: That's right. Our Many Treasures Group members are striving, based on Nichiren's teachings, to realize world peace and to enable all people to become happy. There is no greater or more honorable purpose in life. Furthermore, having such an objective makes each day enjoyable and rewarding. It is the strongest and most admirable way of life.

Inamitsu: That is so true. I'd like to share a story about Jun Tokita, a Soka Gakkai member who operates an assisted care facility for the elderly in Odawara, Kanagawa Prefecture.

IKEDA: I know him well. He's made tremendous contributions to the development of our movement since the early days.

INAMITSU: Even before the new national standards for nursing care went into effect, his assisted care facility became famous throughout Japan for providing first-rate care, balanced nutrition, and so forth for the elderly.

MICHIKAWA: It's considered to be a model of care for the elderly, having pioneered the way for today's assisted care services.

INAMITSU: Mr. Tokita established the facility out of his desire to make a positive contribution to society as a Soka Gakkai member. He's now seventy-eight (in February 2006). Engraving in his heart Nichiren's words "You must not spend your lives in vain and regret it for ten thousand years to come" (WND-1, 622), he has exerted himself wholeheartedly day in and day out not only in Soka Gakkai activities but also for the sake of the facility's residents as the center director. He has a sharp mind and is a model of both physical and mental health.

IKEDA: What a healthy way of life! The Many Treasures Group members, who devote themselves energetically for the well-being of others, society, and the future, are leading the way in our aging society.

INAMITSU: There is one thing you said, President Ikeda, that Mr. Tokita holds dear. That is, "Soka Gakkai activities exist for the sake of society, for the sake of oneself, and for the sake of future generations."

IKEDA: Soka Gakkai activities contain all manner of ways to create value. They contain everything we need to bring our lives to shine, including the promotion of health and long life.

By living out our lives together with the Soka Gakkai, the organization carrying out the Buddha's intent and decree, we will as a matter of course enjoy a healthy life pervaded by the noble virtues of eternity, happiness, true self, and purity.

Life Is a Never-Ending Struggle

IKEDA: Mr. Tokita's story reminds me of Dr. Toynbee's motto—*Laboremus*, which is Latin for "Let's get to work!" It was with this spirit that the historian would sit down to work at his desk at a set time each morning.

NARUMI: The same was true of Dr. Athayde, who was a courageous human rights activist. He wrote an average of two newspaper columns every day of his seventy-year career as a journalist.

IKEDA: Dr. Athayde personally came to meet me when I arrived in Rio de Janeiro in Brazil (in 1993). It was such a warm welcome, making me feel as if I were being greeted by Mr. Toda himself. I'll never forget Dr. Athayde's remarks on that occasion. He said: "I have been working since my late teens. But I have never looked on it as a burden. I just worked as best I could, with all my strength." He also said, "To live is to train oneself, and training leads to victory." Life is a never-ending struggle.

When Dr. Rotblat was once asked about the secret to his health, he replied immediately that remaining active was the key. He also said that the secret to health and youthfulness was never losing one's fighting spirit.

There is no end to the struggle for the happiness of humanity, nor is there an end to the struggle for kosen-rufu. Losing our fighting spirit starts us on a downward spiral of decline.

"Inactivity Saps the Vigor of the Mind"

INAMITSU: Medically speaking, activity is also very important. In the past, hospitalized patients were generally kept in bed for long periods and discouraged from being active. Now, however, they are encouraged to exercise, even very lightly, to keep their physical functions from deteriorating. Even surgical patients are encouraged to sit up as soon as possible to prevent potentially fatal blood clots going to the lungs or other complications.

IKEDA: That's very interesting. Of course, when we're tired, we should rest. At the same time, however, when unused, our bodies and minds age. The same is true of organizations. It's important to keep our organization moving forward. That produces the impetus for further development. If we retreat even the slightest bit, negative influences will take hold and our momentum will stop. Construction is an ongoing, life-and-death struggle, while destruction happens in a moment.

The great Renaissance artist Leonardo da Vinci (1452–1519) said, "Iron rusts when it is not used; stagnant water loses its purity and freezes over with cold; so, too, does inactivity sap the vigor of the mind."[27]

MICHIKAWA: It is just as he says. Spiritual activity produces a spiritual dynamism that age cannot defeat.

IKEDA: The American philosopher Ralph Waldo Emerson (1803–82) wrote, "The one thing in the world, of value, is the active soul."[28] This "active soul," or dynamic spirit, is vibrantly alive in every Soka Gakkai member.

Nichiren says: "Carry through with your faith in the Lotus Sutra. You cannot strike fire from flint if you stop halfway"

(WND-1, 319). I hope that all of our members will continue to make their way through life with this passionate spirit, no matter what their age. Even should you advance in years or fall ill, please never forget: "It is the heart that is important" (WND-1, 1000). As long as the commitment to strive for the sake of others, for the sake of Buddhism and kosen-rufu, burns in your heart, you will remain youthful and glow with health. A fighting spirit is the true fountain of youth and the key to sound health and long life.

7: "We Will Find Perpetual Youth"

IKEDA: Last year (2005), reports of a protein that may extend life spans caused quite a stir.

MICHIKAWA: Yes, the protein klotho. According to a joint Japanese-American research team, mice that were genetically engineered to produce larger than normal amounts of klotho aged more slowly and extended their life spans by about 20 to 30 percent.

NARUMI: Klotho suppresses the production of insulin and inhibits energy metabolism. That, in turn, may reduce reactive oxygen—thought to be one of the main causes of aging—resulting in longer life spans.

INAMITSU: Apparently, some of the mice lived to what would be the equivalent of one hundred twenty in human years. The gene that produces this protein also exists in human beings, so in the future it may well be possible to produce a drug with it that extends human life spans significantly.

NARUMI: But if one really wishes to live a long and healthy life, it's important to take steps to prevent excess production of reactive oxygen. These include eating plenty of vegetables and avoiding such things as overeating, excessive alcohol consumption, overexposure to the sun, stress, and smoking.

IKEDA: People have sought an elixir of eternal youth since ancient times. In one of his writings, Nichiren mentions Tung-fang Shuo, an official in the government of Emperor Wu of the Former Han dynasty in China who went in search of fruit that would ensure longevity (see WND-2, 1008). And in another writing, he mentions the mythical mountain island of P'eng-lai, where legend has it that the elixir of perennial youth and eternal life can be found. He says that just as there are many jewels on P'eng-lai, a cluster of blessings is to be found wherever the votary of the Lotus Sutra dwells (see WND-1, 1070).

The Common Traits of Long-Lived Individuals

INAMITSU: Last year, the oldest person in the world at that time, a Dutch woman of 115, passed away.

IKEDA: Did she attribute her advanced age to anything special?

INAMITSU: Apparently, she ate pickled herring every day to stay healthy.

IKEDA: Mr. Toda [having grown up in Atsuta Village, once a major herring fishing port] also loved eating herring. How does this benefit our health?

MICHIKAWA: Fish oils prevent the accumulation of substances in the brain that are thought to contribute to the development of Alzheimer's disease. Some researchers say that fish oils help prevent inflammation caused by those harmful substances. Fish oils also contain fatty acids that aid in the prevention of arteriosclerosis.

Ikeda: I see. And what about exercise? Does it play a part in enabling us to live long?

Narumi: Almost all regions where a large percentage of people enjoy long life expectancy are mountainous or hilly. Walking along hilly roads seems to be a natural way of maintaining and enhancing one's health.

Michikawa: Walking uphill works the leg and back muscles much more than walking on flat ground. People who get that kind of exercise from the time they are young develop strong hearts and lungs and stay youthful longer.

Inamitsu: It is often said that aging hits the legs first.

Ikeda: People who walk a lot are really winners in health. And footsteps taken for the sake of kosen-rufu in particular resound with supreme victory and hope.

Reading Aloud Stimulates the Brain

Ikeda: Lately, there's been a great deal of attention in Japan on reading aloud as a preventative measure against aging.

Narumi: That's right. Following the written words with our eyes while saying them aloud stimulates numerous areas of the brain.

Inamitsu: That's why reading and reciting the sutra when we do gongyo and chanting vigorously not only polishes our lives on a spiritual level but is also a wonderful workout for our brain.

IKEDA: Reading good writing aloud invigorates the spirit and activates the brain. In particular, reading aloud the writings of Nichiren or articles from SGI publications fills us with inspiration and positive energy. It's also highly beneficial to read such works to children in voices brimming with hope and courage.

The French author George Sand (1804–76) observed, "The brain is a tool that gets rusty without constant, albeit moderate, exercise."[29] Using our voice prevents our brain from growing rusty.

Keeping Our Minds Active

NARUMI: Recently, researchers have found that the production of new brain cells continues even as we age.

IKEDA: That's great news!

MICHIKAWA: It was previously thought that after about age twenty, we lose approximately one hundred thousand brain cells every day. It's been discovered, however, that new cells continue to be produced even in the elderly in the region of the brain called the hippocampus, which is related to memory functions.

NARUMI: In other words, though our bodies may decline, our brains can still remain active.

IKEDA: Such capacities as creativity and wisdom don't necessarily decline with age, do they? Rather, I think many people can testify that those faculties only grow richer with the passing years.

The Struggle Against Aging Is a Struggle Against Fear

Ikeda: Even at ninety-two, the Hong Kong calligrapher and artist Fang Zhaoling (1914–2006) remained active and creative, continuing to pick up her brush to the end of her life. I even received some wonderful calligraphy works from her earlier this year (in January 2006) to celebrate the New Year. Brimming with youthful dynamism, they read: "The Crane Lives One Thousand Years," "Calm and Serene," and "The Pine and The Crane—Symbols of Longevity."[30]

Inamitsu: Madame Fang lost her husband when she was still young and raised their eight children on her own while continuing to be active as a leading painter and calligrapher.

Ikeda: That's true. The Chinese seal that she stamped on those New Year's works consists of four characters that can be read as "Though I age, my vigor increases."

The struggle against aging is really a struggle against the fear to face new challenges. The aging process occurs more rapidly in those who start thinking that they've done enough, who lose the spirit to foster younger people, and who remain attached to the past. Those who keep challenging themselves to the end are the most admirable and youthful of all. Such people are ever young and true victors of life.

Come to think of it, the German writer Johann Wolfgang von Goethe (1749–1832) was eighty when he completed his masterpiece *Faust*.

Narumi: And the great English physicist Isaac Newton (1642–1727) began revising his *Principia* at the age of eighty-two. He retained a passionate thirst for knowledge throughout his life.

Michikawa: The world-renowned cellist Pablo Casals (1876–1973) continued to make important contributions to art and peace with astonishing youthfulness until his death at ninety-six.

Constant Challenge

Ikeda: The Soka Gakkai's founder Tsunesaburo Makiguchi continued advancing and challenging himself until the final moments of his life. He was fifty-seven when he encountered Nichiren Buddhism, and fifty-nine when he founded the Soka Kyoiku Gakkai (Value-Creating Education Society; forerunner of the Soka Gakkai). In his seventies, he was still energetically traveling all the way to Kyushu (the southernmost of Japan's four main islands) on crowded trains to offer personal guidance and share Buddhism with others. He often referred to himself and others of his generation as "We youth."

Inamitsu: The American painter Grandma Moses (1860–1961) didn't start painting in earnest until she was in her late seventies, and she continued to create art until she was over one hundred years old.

Ikeda: About a month before Mr. Makiguchi passed away, he wrote a postcard from his prison cell saying that he "was deeply engaged in reading Kant." Such passionate seeking spirit and thirst for knowledge are no doubt the source of youthfulness.

Narumi: I'd like to ask you, President Ikeda, to talk about the significance of the Buddhist teaching of perennial youth and eternal life.

Ikeda: First of all, this principle does not mean of course that we never age or die. It refers to our state of life, our life force. The Lotus Sutra says, "If a person who has an illness is able to hear this sutra, then his illness will be wiped out and he will know neither old age or death" (LSOC, 330). And the Daishonin writes, "If we consider the power of the Lotus Sutra, we will find perpetual youth and eternal life before our eyes" (WND-1, 413).

In other words, we are promised that, if we believe in and uphold the Mystic Law, we will never be defeated by illness, we can forever advance through life with a youthful spirit regardless of our age, and we can establish an eternal and indestructible state of happiness. This is nothing extraordinary or supernatural. The precious members of the Many Treasures Group, who are always vibrantly active, are a perfect example of such living.

A Satisfying and Fulfilling Time of Life

Narumi: People generally think of aging in negative terms.

Inamitsu: This is reflected in people's concerns about the social security system and our rapidly graying society, I think.

Ikeda: In a certain respect, it's only natural that people dislike growing old, for it makes us think of the inevitable reality of death.

Narumi: Because aging ends in death, people naturally fear and abhor it.

Ikeda: Yes. But each period of life has its own distinct and precious value.

What is the true significance of aging? It is not a time to look back with nostalgic longing on our youth. I believe it is the climax, the period of life that should be the most satisfying and fulfilling, the time when we shine with the brilliance and glory of a magnificent sunset. It's not a period of gloom and sadness. As Victor Hugo (1802–85) said, "There is something of the dawn in happy old age."[31]

Unfortunately, however, society today has averted its gaze from the fundamental reality of death, and in the process has lost sight of the golden value of old age.

INAMITSU: It's just as you discussed in your lecture at Harvard, titled "Mahayana Buddhism and Twenty-First-Century Civilization."

You said: "Modern civilization has attempted to ignore death. We have diverted our gaze from this most fundamental of concerns as we try to drive death into the shadows. For many people living today, death is the mere absence of life; it is blankness; it is the void. Life is identified with all that is good: with being, rationality, and light. In contrast, death is perceived as evil, as nothingness, and as the dark and irrational. Only the negative perception of death prevails."[32]

MICHIKAWA: With the development of modern medicine, there are more hospitals than ever before, medical technology and treatment have advanced remarkably, and reliance on hospital care has increased. As a result, care for the dying has shifted from the home to hospitals. In 1951, the number of people in Japan who died in their homes was a little over 80 percent, whereas in 2002, that number declined to 13 percent, demonstrating that most people are opting to spend their final days in hospitals or some other kind of care facilities. We depend more and more heavily on physicians and medicine, and death has all but disappeared from our daily experience.

IKEDA: Nichiren encourages us to "first of all learn about death, and then about other things" (WND-2, 759). We must not avert our gaze from death but face it head-on and come to terms with it. If we can do that, old age will come to be appreciated in its own right and its true value will surely start to shine.

INAMITSU: Toward that end, a solid understanding of life and death is crucial.

IKEDA: That's right. From the Buddhist perspective of the eternity of life, death is just a departure into the next phase of life.

Nichiren describes the Mystic Law as "the great lantern that illuminates the long night of the sufferings of birth and death" (WND-1, 1038). Those who embrace the eternal Mystic Law are not afraid of death. They are not worried or troubled by it. They are able to freely walk the journey of life, experiencing a state of mind in which both life and death are a joy.

Nichiren Buddhism teaches the fundamental method for transforming a life bound by the four sufferings of birth, aging, sickness, and death into a joyous existence of eternity, happiness, true self, and purity.

Cherishing the Elderly

IKEDA: Returning to the subject of aging, what specific abilities actually improve with age?

MICHIKAWA: Generally, memory and concentration decline, but our judgment and ability to process information, which are based on a rich fund of knowledge and experience, often grow keener with age.

IKEDA: In other words, we acquire what is often called the "wisdom of age." In fact, American anthropologists recently came out with research on this very subject.

INAMITSU: That is correct. Some thirty thousand years ago, the number of adults reaching the age of thirty, which was a senior age at the time, began to rise dramatically. This surge in numbers of elderly humans is believed to be the key to our evolution. The older generation played a huge role in our social development.

IKEDA: After raising their own children, elders helped raise their grandchildren, passing on to them important knowledge and skills. The research concluded that those families tended to prosper.

Basically, cherishing the elderly, who have contributed greatly to society, is the way to eternal prosperity. Nichiren writes:

> King Wen of the Chou dynasty was victorious in battle because he took care to provide for elderly people. During the thirty-seven reigns spanning eight hundred years in which his descendants ruled, there were some incidents of misgovernment, but on the whole the Chou dynasty prospered due to that fundamental virtue. (WND-1, 916)

NARUMI: In another of his writings, Nichiren refers to a country called "Abandoning the Old" (WND-2, 599).

Ikeda: Yes. It was a country where the elderly were cast aside in order to reduce the number of mouths to feed. According to a Buddhist scripture (the Miscellaneous Treasury Sutra), this inhuman practice was eventually abolished because of one clever old man. It seems that the man's son, a government minister, could not bear to part with him, so he broke the law and cared for him in secret. Then one day the country faced a terrible crisis and no one knew what to do. The minister turned to his father for advice and the latter ended up saving the day. The king thereupon changed the laws to ensure that the elderly were treated with reverence.

Shakyamuni taught that those who treasure and respect the elderly will enjoy long lives and will come to shine with greater beauty, joy, and strength. A society that respects the elderly is a society that respects life, and it will become a place that brims with the joy of life itself.

"The Old Are More Beautiful Than the Young"

Inamitsu: I think that a mature and fully developed character is the true gift of the elderly.

Ikeda: I agree. Nichiren Daishonin speaks of the leader of the Bodhisattvas of the Earth as "a venerable old man called Bodhisattva Superior Practices" (WND-1, 605). This is a reference to the description of Bodhisattva Superior Practices in the Lotus Sutra as "the hundred-year-old man" (LSOC, 261–62). Comparing the venerable appearance of Bodhisattva Superior Practices to Shakyamuni, the sutra says that the former is like a hundred-year-old man while the latter is like a youth of twenty-five. The sutra further describes these Bodhisattvas of the Earth as richly imbued with noble virtues, being "firm in will," "in no way timid," "clever at difficult questions and answers," "upright in dignity and virtue," and having "firmly cultivated persevering minds" (LSOC, 263).

The great American poet Walt Whitman (1819–92) praised the elderly as well, singing, "The young are beautiful—but the old are more beautiful than the young."[33] Indeed, nothing is more inspiring and refreshing than older people who have lived long and shine with years of hard-won experience and wisdom.

MICHIKAWA: In the old days in Japan, there was a person known as "the elder" in every community. Such people were treasure troves of wisdom, and they traditionally acted as mediators to resolve disputes or conflicts in families or among members of the community.

IKEDA: They were always on hand to offer sound advice.

The members of the Many Treasures Group are also considered to be good advisers not only in their families but in their communities and on the front lines of kosen-rufu.

In one of his writings, Nichiren praises one such pillar of the community, saying, "He was as wise as he was advanced in years, and he enjoyed robust health and commanded the esteem of the local people" (WND-1, 1007). It was just such predecessors of the Many Treasures Group who protected Nichiren during his exile on Sado.

INAMITSU: The wonderful thing about the Many Treasures Group members is that they are earnestly putting to use all the ability and wisdom they have gained through forging their faith over the years in helping their friends, their communities, society, and the youth of the next generation.

"May We Use Our Long Lives to Save Living Beings"

Ikeda: A passage in the Lotus Sutra states, "Our wish is that . . . we may use our long lives to save living beings" (LSOC, 280). This should be the vow of all who uphold the Mystic Law. The important thing is to have the bodhisattva spirit to live long, so that, based on the Mystic Law, we can make use of our experience and wisdom not just for ourselves but to support and encourage others.

In this respect, the Many Treasures Group is a model organization for a graying society.

Michikawa: Yes, society is going to have to start looking at aging as one aspect of each person's identity and finding ways of making valuable use of this reality.

In Japan today (as of February 2006), there are twenty-five million people over the age of sixty-five, of which only 13 to 16 percent need special nursing care. The majority, though they may have some health problem, are relatively well and eager to live, and they have wonderful abilities that they have acquired over the years. If we can find a way to make use of the energy of our older population and link it to the growth and development of our communities and society at large, the future will be bright.

Narumi: The graying of our society will continue. Because of this, some are beginning to suggest that the official age for determining senior citizenship should be raised from sixty-five to seventy-five. We are beginning to recognize that many who in the past were regarded as old because of their age are actually still quite youthful and energetic.

A "Seniors Renaissance" Starting From the Many Treasures Group

IKEDA: That's only to be expected.

In the next decade, the 6.8 million members of the baby boom generation in Japan will move from their sixties into their seventies. The fact that this generation that has been the engine of postwar Japan's prosperity remains active will have a major effect on the definition and understanding of old age in our society. In that context, our Many Treasures Group members, as exemplars of our increasingly long-lived society, have a noble mission to carry out a "Seniors Renaissance" by restoring value to the aging process.

8: Dealing With Dementia

IKEDA: "In none of his tendencies has he come to a standstill; he is still learning and learning—a man endowed with perpetual, imperishable youth."[34] This was a description of the great German writer Johann Wolfgang von Goethe when he was in his late seventies. As a "perpetual youth," he continued to impart limitless hope and inspiration to others. We should all aspire to live the same way.

INAMITSU: Yes. Though we may grow a bit forgetful as we age, we should still move forward with a youthful spirit. As Nichiren writes, "You will grow younger, and your good fortune will accumulate" (WND-1, 464).

IKEDA: Is forgetfulness always a part of aging?

INAMITSU: It seems to be. Most people begin to experience memory loss after their forties. They start to forget things they have done, like what they ate for breakfast the previous day.

MICHIKAWA: That degree of memory loss, which the individual is aware of, is not usually a problem. But forgetting the very fact that one has eaten breakfast may point to some form of dementia, such as Alzheimer's disease. One characteristic of this illness is being completely oblivious to one's own loss of memory.

NARUMI: For example, a person may insist that they haven't eaten a meal even when they have, or start fabricating stories out of thin air. Failing to address such symptoms could severely interfere with daily functioning.

IKEDA: Why does dementia happen?

MICHIKAWA: Simply put, dementia results when, for one reason or another, the nerve cells in the brain malfunction, disrupting neural processes. This leads to the impairment of cognitive or intellectual functions, such as memory, judgment, and comprehension.

NARUMI: At present, some 1.6 million patients in Japan are suffering from dementia, and it is predicted that the number will rise to three million in twenty years.

IKEDA: What is the fundamental cause of dementia?

INAMITSU: The main form of dementia in Japan used to be vascular dementia. This is caused by strokes, which disrupt the supply of blood in the brain, resulting in brain dysfunction.

MICHIKAWA: Recently, however, the number of people diagnosed with Alzheimer's disease in Japan is on the rise, and it is becoming the predominant form of dementia. This is thought to be due in part to the Westernization of the Japanese diet. Improved medical technology also means that people are being accurately diagnosed. Vascular dementia, on the other hand, is on the decline owing to an increase in preventative measures against various lifestyle-related diseases such as high blood pressure.

Alzheimer's Disease

Ikeda: Could you tell us a little about Alzheimer's disease?

Michikawa: Alzheimer's is named after German psychiatrist Alois Alzheimer (1864–1915), who discovered [in 1906] that the accumulation of a certain protein in the brain can obstruct the functioning of nerve cells and lead to dementia. Research in recent years has taught us a great deal more about its causes and mechanisms.

Ikeda: Does that protein accumulate in everyone's brains?

Michikawa: From about the mid-forties, it does gradually accumulate in the brains of all people, and as such is a part of the general aging process. But the mere accumulation of this protein does not cause Alzheimer's. It can take as long as twenty years for symptoms of Alzheimer's to appear. And not everyone develops Alzheimer's.

Ikeda: I see. So the important thing is for someone suffering from telltale signs of Alzheimer's to see a doctor.

Narumi: That's right. It should be noted, however, that memory loss can also be caused by things other than Alzheimer's, including depression and metabolic or neurological disorders. At the same time, early diagnosis of Alzheimer's makes it possible for patients to receive treatment that reduces symptoms, while also enabling their families to prepare for dealing with the illness.

Michikawa: Everyone occasionally forgets the names of people or objects, or where they've put things. There's no need to worry about such memory lapses unless they start to escalate dramatically.

INAMITSU: In some cases, people may lose their sense of time or fail to recognize familiar places or streets, or remember what season it is.

IKEDA: That sounds serious.

NARUMI: Other warning signs are sudden changes in a person's interests and favorite things—for example, no longer wanting to watch a favorite TV program.

MICHIKAWA: As the condition intensifies, the individual may experience a decline in motivation or emotional control, or start exhibiting psychological disturbances such as delusions or paranoia. They may also wander off on occasion or become prone to violent outbursts, which can make caring for them very challenging.

The Twilight Years

INAMITSU: The well-known Japanese novelist Sawako Ariyoshi (1931–84), with whom you have met, President Ikeda, addressed the subject of aging and senility in her pioneering 1972 bestseller *The Twilight Years*.

IKEDA: I have many fond memories of Sawako Ariyoshi. We met on eight occasions. Though an influential literary figure, she was not in the least bit self-important or conceited. Her spirit shone with the unflagging resolve of a great writer dedicated to investigating life and the human condition.

NARUMI: It was Ms. Ariyoshi who delivered your initial correspondence from Chinese Premier Zhou Enlai (1898–1976), wasn't it?

IKEDA: That's right. It was in May 1966.

She said: "I have a message from Premier Zhou Enlai. He would like to invite you to visit China some time and asked me to convey this invitation to you."

It is extremely unfortunate that she passed away at the youthful age of fifty-three. But her daughter Tamao Ariyoshi has inherited her spirit and is also a talented writer.

INAMITSU: *The Twilight Years* vividly depicts a woman's struggles to care for her father-in-law suffering from dementia. While the woman devotes herself with tireless devotion, her husband, who sees his own future reflected in his father's condition, doesn't lift a finger to help.

MICHIKAWA: I think the son avoids dealing with his father's illness out of fear that the same is going to happen to him someday. He is representative of many people today who try to ignore the realities of illness and death.

IKEDA: About six months after *The Twilight Years* was published, I met with Ms. Ariyoshi in Kyoto. At that time, she said: "Old age is one of the sober realities of human life. The sufferings of growing old have nothing to do with capitalism or socialism. All people, whether they be capitalists or laborers, have to grow old." She also said that she took on this subject because she believed it was one that she, as a writer, could not avoid.

She certainly had foresight. In Japan's now rapidly graying

society, her words are even more significant. The themes that Ms. Ariyoshi took up in her writing—the meaning of old age and death, and how we should live our lives—are becoming more important every day.

Caregiving at Home

IKEDA: Incidentally, President Makiguchi cared for his bedridden elderly mother-in-law.

NARUMI: I didn't know that.

IKEDA: He used to carry her on his back to the bathroom and help her bathe. Dr. Michikawa, do you have any personal experience with such caregiving?

MICHIKAWA: When I had just begun practicing as a doctor, my grandmother was diagnosed with Alzheimer's disease. My mother took care of her for about three years at our home.

INAMITSU: How old was your grandmother?

MICHIKAWA: She was in her eighties, and my mother was in her fifties. My mother was working at the time, so she had to be away from home during the day. I know she worried whenever she had to leave my grandmother at home alone.

IKEDA: Her efforts are now being reflected in your research. In caring for others, the important thing is to try not to shoulder it alone. It's crucial to get advice and help from a variety of people.

INAMITSU: The understanding of the entire family and the support of others are indispensable in caring for the infirm at home. Each member of the family needs to have a clear-cut role and share the work involved. I particularly think that men should be aware of the efforts in this regard of their wives and mothers, on whom most of the burden tends to fall, remembering to lend a helping hand and show their appreciation.

IKEDA: Nichiren praised and encouraged the lay nun Toki (the wife of Toki Jonin), who was caring for her elderly mother-in-law. In a letter to her, Nichiren writes that Toki Jonin said he was grateful that she gave his mother such attentive care and that he would never be able to forget this in any lifetime to come (see WND-1, 656). These words must have been a great comfort to the lay nun Toki.

NARUMI: When caregiving at home continues for an extended period, or when there are complications, such as a patient who keeps wandering off, families should consult with professionals. They can also make use of various public or private care services or facilities. There's no need to hesitate; they exist to be used.

MICHIKAWA: Fortunately, my grandmother did not leave the house and wander around the streets. But in the evening, she would say "I want to go home," even though she was home. Once, she hid in the closet, and we all had to search the house for her. She would also do things like put her possessions away and then, forgetting she had done so, tell us that she had lost them. I remember once she kept insisting that some weeds in the yard were delicious vegetables and telling my mother that she wanted to eat them.

INAMITSU: What did your mother do?

MICHIKAWA: At first she tried telling my grandmother that they were just weeds and she couldn't eat them, but since my grandmother remained unconvinced, my mother finally boiled the weeds and allowed her to taste them. Of course, they were bitter and tough and she didn't want to eat them, and from then on she stopped insisting that they were delicious vegetables.

IKEDA: Gaining a person's understanding is better than just telling them no, and winning their consent is better than pleading with them. When we make such efforts for people suffering from dementia, they feel that we care about them and understand them, even though they might not necessarily show it. It gives them comfort and reassurance.

Avoid Sudden Changes to the Environment or Daily Routine

INAMITSU: I agree. I once made a mistake along those lines. In the summer of 2005, my ninety-two-year-old mother had to be hospitalized for dehydration.

NARUMI: Many times hospitalization can trigger or worsen dementia in elderly patients, so you must have been very worried.

INAMITSU: I was. While my mother was in the hospital, I spoke to her a great deal, trying to keep her mind active. Two days after she left the hospital, I used our nursing-care insurance to buy her a new bed that would make it easier to care for her. I also hung up photos on the walls of her bedroom, thinking it would brighten the space and lift her spirits.

That night, however, after we had finished a conversation

in her bedroom, she said: "I think I'll go to bed now. Can you take me to my room?"

IKEDA: I guess it's true that one should avoid making sudden changes in the environment or routine of elderly people.

INAMITSU: Yes. To me, they didn't seem like such big changes. Anyway, I tried to calm her, telling her that it was her bedroom and that the only thing that was different was the bed. But as soon as the words were out of my mouth, I regretted having corrected her, thinking it could make the situation worse. Fortunately, however, she realized that what I was saying was true and she went to sleep in her new bed. She never showed any signs of dementia after that one incident.

IKEDA: Anyone might be taken aback when confronted with remarks or actions that are unexpected or out of context. I think it's important in such situations, though, not to panic or lose one's temper but to just accept the other person's reaction with a smile.

Feelings of anxiety and alienation are always just beneath the surface in illness. Caring for people struggling with illness must start from the desire to listen to their pain and understand their suffering.

A Balanced Diet

IKEDA: Let's talk about what people can do to stave off dementia. First, how about diet?

INAMITSU: A balanced diet is of course crucial. There are several important foods and food groups that were common in the traditional Japanese diet but tend to be lacking in the Japanese diet today—that is, legumes, sesame seeds, seaweed, vegetables, fish, mushrooms, and root vegetables. The traditional Japanese diet is well balanced and helps prevent all kinds of diseases, both of the brain and the rest of the body.

NARUMI: To avoid vascular dementia, it's important to reduce salt intake. Too much sodium contributes to high blood pressure and hardening of the arteries (arteriosclerosis), which can cause strokes that lead to the onset of dementia.

IKEDA: As was mentioned earlier, some fish oils help prevent the accumulation in the brain of the protein that causes Alzheimer's, in addition to fighting hardening of the arteries.

MICHIKAWA: Some studies have indeed shown that to be true. To prevent the accumulation of reactive oxygen species that can damage nerve cells, people should also eat fruits and vegetables rich in vitamin E, vitamin C, polyphenol, and other antioxidants.

IKEDA: Is there anything else to watch out for?

NARUMI: I would recommend people to give up smoking. Smoking can damage the blood vessels in the brain. Compared with nonsmokers, smokers are said to have twice the risk of cerebral infarction and three times the risk of cerebral hemorrhage.

THE BENEFITS OF WALKING

IKEDA: Exercise is also important in preventing dementia, isn't it?

MICHIKAWA: Yes, it is. Exercise improves circulation, stimulates the brain, and also has a positive effect on emotional health.

NARUMI: Exercise also plays a crucial role in preventing high blood pressure and arteriosclerosis. Moderate exercise keeps the legs and back strong, but strenuous exercise can have a negative effect.

INAMITSU: I recommend walking for about thirty minutes a day. The best way to walk is to stand tall and take long strides, moving the arms at the same time. Working up a light sweat is ideal.

IKEDA: Early Buddhist practitioners used to engage in a walking practice after meditation, as a form of exercise. An early Buddhist text lists five positive effects of this exercise: (1) physical conditioning, (2) reducing sickness, (3) improving digestion, (4) promoting clear thinking, and (5) strengthening the will.[35]

NARUMI: These are quite similar to the benefits of walking noted by modern medicine.

IKEDA: In other words, someone who's always walking, always on the move, will be in vigorous mental and physical health. In that respect, Soka Gakkai activities are the best health regimen there is. Attending meetings, visiting friends to encourage them, and going out to share Nichiren's teaching with others—all of these involve activity. And they are all a form of contributive service—for the sake of Buddhism, for the sake of one's friends, and for the sake of society at large.

It could be said that Mr. Makiguchi led the kosen-rufu

movement on foot. He walked so much in his effort to share Buddhism with others that his wooden sandals were always worn down to the nubs.

NARUMI: Dr. Unger also emphasizes the importance of walking.

IKEDA: That's right. And he also stresses that in order to live long, healthy lives, we need not only physical exercise but also some sort of spiritual exercise, such as deepening our faith and conviction.

Nichiren writes, "If one lights a fire for others, one will brighten one's own way" (WND-2, 1060). Every step we take for kosen-rufu increases our good fortune, contributes positively to society, and expands our circle of friends. Working for kosen-rufu is the supreme path of happiness and health.

INAMITSU: That's the joy of doing Soka Gakkai activities.

The Importance of a Good Nap

IKEDA: If your days are spent in fulfilling activity, you will enjoy sound sleep. Sleep is very important when it comes to keeping the mind active and alert.

MICHIKAWA: Studies have shown that taking a brief daily nap of less than thirty minutes can also help prevent Alzheimer's disease.

IKEDA: Until his death at age ninety-two, my friend the American entrepreneur Armand Hammer always took a short nap each day. Sleep is indeed the best medicine. Elderly people in particular need to make an effort to get enough sleep so they don't become overtired. They should make time to rest in order to keep themselves in the best condition.

Incidentally, are there certain types of people who are less susceptible to dementia?

MICHIKAWA: Some studies show that writers and artists are less likely to experience dementia. It may be because they are constantly using their minds, whether it be reading newspapers and books, writing, or engaging in the creative processes of bringing new paintings or other works of art into being. Such people are constantly expanding their neural networks and strengthening the connections between neurons in the brain, which help prevent Alzheimer's disease.

IKEDA: I see. They are always using and exercising their minds, which helps prevent dementia. That's another reason for reading good books that stimulate the mind.

A Positive Outlook

NARUMI: I think it can also be said that people with a positive outlook tend not to experience dementia. I'm talking about people who are able to use their various struggles and stresses as the driving force for moving forward.

MICHIKAWA: Studies have shown that people with a negative attitude are more likely to be susceptible to various forms of dementia. Withdrawn, silent, passive people are at a greater risk.

IKEDA: In Buddhism, we speak of this realm in which we live as the saha world. Nichiren states, "Saha means a world in which one must exercise forbearance and learn to endure" (OTT, 169). In such a world, stress is an inescapable part of life. But the Lotus Sutra teaches that this world is also a place where "living beings enjoy themselves at ease" (LSOC, 272). In other words, when we manifest the life state of Buddhahood, this world of endurance becomes a place of happiness and joy.

Referring to this passage of the Lotus Sutra, Mr. Toda used to say, "Human beings were born in this world to enjoy life, not to suffer." If we chant vigorously and bring forth powerful life force and rich wisdom, we will never be deadlocked. We can overcome all of life's challenges joyfully, like a surfer riding a wave. We can establish an unshakable life state and existence of eternity, happiness, true self, and purity. That's the purpose of faith.

INAMITSU: That's an indestructible state of being in which we can savor boundless and absolute freedom, isn't it?

I think humor and laughter are also very important in life. The American authors of a book on longevity say, "[Humor] encourages and enables our minds to keep active, which is one of the most important defenses we have against aging."[36]

IKEDA: I agree. The question is whether we have the emotional and mental resilience to respond to all kinds of stress with a positive outlook and the self-confidence that we can overcome it. A life of continual challenge is truly fulfilling and hopeful.

Nichiren calmly faced the life-threatening persecutions he met, saying: "I feel immeasurable delight" (WND-1, 386); "[These troubles] are no more to me than dust before the wind" (WND-1, 280); and "What greater joy could there be?" (WND-1, 767). The ultimate purpose of Buddhism is to allow us to feel ever more joyful the greater our difficulties become.

No matter what our age, we should continue upholding such a courageous and optimistic spirit, making our way through life cheerfully and confidently.

Remaining Active and Interested

MICHIKAWA: Having others to talk to can also help prevent dementia in that it provides mental stimulation. In one of the studies relating to dementia I mentioned earlier, it was found that many of those who experienced dementia displayed a varying degree of antisocial traits and such behavioral symptoms as stubbornness, rigidity, self-centeredness, irritability, and uncommunicativeness.

IKEDA: That's an important point. In his later years, Goethe said: "It is not good for man to be alone, and especially to work alone. He needs sympathy and suggestion to do anything well."[37] Retaining such an openhearted spirit even in old age was the secret to the youthful vigor of Goethe's creativity.

Many people tend to become apathetic or socially withdrawn as they age. As I quoted earlier, "The true evil is not the weakening of the body, but the indifference of the soul."[38]

INAMITSU: That's true. I think that happens more often to older people who are living alone. Such apathy can lead to the development of dementia. It's important, therefore, that we reach out to and spend time talking with the elderly in our community.

NARUMI: Researchers have found that the lively back and forth of conversation, which requires our quick assessment and response to the words and reactions of those we're talking to, stimulates the brain. Communicating and interacting with others instead of shutting ourselves off is the key to keeping our brains healthy.

IKEDA: This means that there is scientific support for the importance of dialogue. Of course, even in dialogue, it is difficult to communicate one's true feelings or fully understand what the other person is thinking. But that's precisely why interacting with others strengthens us and enriches our lives. It also keeps our brain active and stimulated.

Please don't close yourselves off from others. Instead, break through your timidity and self-consciousness and go out to meet and speak with others. I hope you follow this most human path to the end of your days.

Each Day of Old Age Is Priceless

NARUMI: A look at people who are still living relatively active lives in their eighties and beyond shows that many of them are taking part in some sort of volunteer activity and have numerous friends.

IKEDA: Continuing to make vigorous efforts to contribute to the well-being of one's friends and one's community even as one grows old—this is a wonderful model of a healthy life. Such a life has real fulfillment. The Edo-period scholar Kaibara Ekiken (1630–1714) observed that each day of old age is priceless.[39] How can we spend our golden years in a productive, fulfilling manner? How can we use them wisely? This is the most important issue in a graying society. It is a matter of the essential quality of life.

Nichiren writes, "It is better to live a single day with honor than to live to 120 and die in disgrace" (WND-1, 851). Of course, we all wish to live as long as possible, but even more significant is what we accomplish in the amount of time we have. What kind of contribution have we left behind? How many people have we helped become happy? How much have we elevated our state of life?

With each passing year, I continue to work hard for the sake of kosen-rufu and my precious fellow members, striving to accomplish a week or month's worth of effort each day. The French philosopher Jean-Jacques Rousseau (1712–78) wrote, "The man who has lived the most is not he who has counted the most years but he who has most felt life."[40] To devote oneself to the welfare of others and society and be able to say each day, "I have won, I have accomplished something worthwhile," gives one a sense of fulfillment and deep satisfaction that is eternal and everlasting. This is the most valuable life there is.

Inspiration Keeps Us Young

Narumi: Research has also shown that about 80 percent of elderly people who are still active have someone in their lives who encourages and supports them, and 70 percent have someone whom they encourage and support.

Ikeda: The Soka Gakkai is just such a realm of mutual encouragement and support. Every day, members young and old are encouraging and supporting one another. It's a beautiful organization. We are extremely fortunate.

Inamitsu: I agree wholeheartedly. As we age, it's easy to become apathetic and withdrawn, as well as lose our ability to feel inspired. But Soka Gakkai activities consistently provide us with inspiration.

IKEDA: It is indeed true that people who remain interested and curious about things around them are always youthful. They are vital and shining.

INAMITSU: I think that people who maintain the ability to feel joy and be inspired, and who have a sense of appreciation, are also unlikely to experience dementia.

IKEDA: In that sense, Soka Gakkai activities can be seen as a means for staving off dementia. Each day, members read Nichiren's writings and various Soka Gakkai publications, which keeps their mental faculties active. When they face some problem, rather than worry about it, they challenge it with their Buddhist practice and then share their experience with their friends. They are also moved and inspired when they see their friends revitalizing their own lives. In this way, they are able to keep every aspect of their lives—body, mind, and spirit—engaged. Nothing we do in the course of our Soka Gakkai activities is wasted.

"Strengthen Your Faith Day by Day"

MICHIKAWA: That is very true. If I could add just one more characteristic of those less likely to succumb to dementia, it is having a purpose in life and a strong desire to continue improving oneself.

Another study, though it doesn't deal directly with dementia, has shown that people with a youthful appearance and those who have some sort of responsibility at their jobs or in their communities are more youthful, both physically and physiologically. If we wish to remain youthful and healthy, we mustn't withdraw from life or the world. I think this study shows the importance of having a purpose in life.

INAMITSU: It's certainly the case that people who retire without having given any thought to their life after retirement tend to suffer in terms of their health.

IKEDA: There is no retirement when it comes to leading a fulfilling life. The world-renowned economist John Kenneth Galbraith (1908–2006) lived to be ninety-seven. When I first met Dr. Galbraith, he was eighty-one. I remember he said at that time that he believed that the older one becomes, the more important it is to keep learning.[41]

INAMITSU: There are many older people with a powerful drive to learn and improve themselves among the students of the Soka University correspondence program of which I'm a faculty member. Asako Soeda from Kanagawa is now eighty-three years old (as of February 2006). She started her correspondence studies at the age of sixty-five as a special student without a high school diploma, and so far she has earned degrees from both the Law Department and the Education Department. She has visual and other physical disabilities, but she has always studied with the determination to work ten times as hard as anyone else. Saying that there is still much that she wants to learn, she will begin a course in the Faculty of Human Studies this April (2006).

IKEDA: I deeply respect her incredible commitment to her personal growth. Mr. Toda often used to say that the final stage of our life is the most crucial.

Instead of lamenting that our time is drawing to a close, we should cause the bright sun of our mission to rise in our hearts, firmly believing that a new chapter of life is just beginning. Nichiren urges us, "Strengthen your faith day by day and month after month" (WND-1, 997). Indeed, we must continually strive onward.

Savoring a Life of Eternity, Happiness, True Self, and Purity

Narumi: There's a lovely poem by an elderly American woman describing the joys of old age:

> *Age is the top of the mountain*
> *Nearer the sky so blue*
> *A long hard climb*
> *A bit of fatigue*
> *But oh—what a*
> *wonderful view!*[42]

Ikeda: What an inspiring poem!

Nichiren writes of the state of life that those who have worked hard for kosen-rufu will experience after death, saying:

> Chant Nam-myoho-renge-kyo. Continue your practice without backsliding until the final moment of your life, and when that time comes, behold! When you climb the mountain of perfect enlightenment and gaze around you in all directions, then to your amazement you will see that the entire realm of phenomena is the Land of Tranquil Light. The ground will be of lapis lazuli, and the eight paths will be set apart by golden ropes. Four kinds of flowers will fall from the heavens, and music will resound in the air. All Buddhas and bodhisattvas will be present in complete joy, caressed by the breezes of eternity, happiness, true self, and purity. The time is fast approaching when

we too will count ourselves among their number. (WND-I, 760–61)

When they die, people who have dedicated their lives to the Mystic Law will savor such an eternal state of eternity, happiness, true self, and purity. Mr. Toda also used to say, "If you carry out your faith wholeheartedly, life itself will become a great joy and you will without fail experience a state of absolute happiness."

Let us joyfully surmount all challenges that come our way as we aim for the great summit of victory in our lives and kosen-rufu. There is no more exhilarating life or better health regimen.

9: The Key to Good Health Care

Ikeda: Ms. O'Connell, thank you for joining us all the way from the United States. I'm glad to see you looking so well.

Gene Marie O'Connell: President Ikeda, I am overjoyed to have this opportunity to meet with you.

Dr. Shuhei Morita[43]**:** Ms. O'Connell is one of the first women to become the CEO of a general hospital in the United States.

Ikeda: Yes, I know. You're the CEO of San Francisco General Hospital.[44]

O'Connell: That's right. I've been in my position since 1998.

Morita: In addition to your professional duties, you are also working on the front lines of kosen-rufu as a district leader.

O'Connell: I owe everything I am today to the SGI and you, President Ikeda.

Ikeda: You were a nurse for many years. In Japan, you would be a member of our women's division nurses group, the Shirakaba Group. The fact that you were selected for your present position because of your contributions as a nurse is truly respectable.

MORITA: We're also joined today by Ms. Hayashi, leader of the young women's division Shirakaba Group.

SHINKO HAYASHI: I'm very happy to be here.

IKEDA: You were appointed leader of the group this January [2006], weren't you, Ms. Hayashi?

HAYASHI: That's right.

IKEDA: Your mother, Eiko, was also the leader of the Shirakaba Group when it was first established (in 1969). I will never forget her. She was a dear comrade in faith. You have followed in her footsteps by pursuing the noble career of nursing. I know she would be very proud of you.

HAYASHI: A pivotal moment in my life was when you warmly encouraged me at the Tokyo Soka Elementary School after my mother's death.

IKEDA: It's wonderful to see bright and confident women, exemplary leaders for an age of women and of life, actively taking the stage in Japan and around the world.

MORITA: We also have many outstanding women active in the doctors division.

Hope Lengthens Life

MORITA: I'd like to start by asking Ms. O'Connell to tell us how she encountered Nichiren Buddhism.

IKEDA: I'm sure your story will inspire members worldwide, so, by all means, please share it with us.

O'CONNELL: Gladly! As you mentioned earlier, I am currently the CEO of San Francisco General Hospital. Interestingly, I first encountered Nichiren Buddhism in the waiting room of that same hospital thirty-two years ago (in 1974). I was twenty-eight years old. I had recently divorced and was having a hard time supporting my two young children. The minimal welfare benefits I was receiving were just barely enough to scrape by on. My children were frequently ill, and I was always taking them to the hospital.

IKEDA: It must have been a very trying time in your life.

O'CONNELL: Yes. While I sat waiting for the doctor to see my children, I often wondered what would become of me. One day, while lost in such thoughts, a woman sitting nearby spoke to me. She was an SGI member.

IKEDA: It seems that encounter marked an important turning point in your life.

O'CONNELL: It did. I'll never forget the warm, family-like atmosphere of the first SGI discussion meeting I attended. I felt like everyone there really cared about me, and it gave me real peace of mind. After encountering the SGI and finding hope for the future through my Buddhist practice, I decided to fulfill my childhood dream of becoming a nurse and entered a university that offered free tuition at the time.

IKEDA: Nichiren Buddhism is indeed a philosophy of hope. Nichiren writes, "Those who believe in the Lotus Sutra are as if in winter, but winter always turns to spring" (WND-1, 536). As symbolized by these words, those who live out their lives based on the Mystic Law will never be deadlocked. They can surmount the most difficult of trials and carry on with even greater hope. People with hope in their hearts are always vibrant and energetic. A Buddhist scripture says that hope has the power to nourish the body and lengthen life.

MORITA: Studies have shown that older people with a positive attitude tend to remain robust. Hope is a "fountain of youth" for both body and mind.

IKEDA: Even those who are struggling with illness need to have hope in their lives. Though they may be bedridden, they mustn't let that defeat them. Having great struggles means we have a great mission, a great purpose in life. When one falls ill, that, too, is part of one's mission. As Nichiren says, "Could not this illness . . . be the Buddha's design?" (WND-1, 937). I hope that all those battling illness will win over it, confident that they have a wonderful mission to demonstrate the tremendous power of the Mystic Law.

SERVING OTHERS AS A WAY TO HEALTH

O'CONNELL: SGI members constantly kept the flame of hope burning in my heart. My life was still quite difficult in the early days of my practice, and I remember once when some Japanese women's division members encouraged me with a gift of homemade rice balls. I didn't really know anything about Japanese culture at the time and had never seen a rice ball before. I'll never forget how delicious they were—it was the taste of the women's sincerity.

HAYASHI: I also decided to become a nurse because of the warm encouragement of my seniors in faith. I was in the third grade when my mother died of malignant melanoma, a type of skin cancer. Afterward, members of the nurses group told me how my mother had dedicated her life to nursing, and when I was a junior high school student, I decided to follow in her footsteps and become a nurse myself.

IKEDA: I see. The earnest support of fellow members, especially in the women's division, is truly wonderful. Wishing solely to help others grow and become happy, members strive selflessly without any thought of their own personal gain. There is no nobler life than that. The essence of good health surely lies in this bodhisattva spirit and bodhisattva action.

O'CONNELL: I first met you, President Ikeda, the year after I started practicing. I was on the first aid team at the All-America General Meeting that took place in Hawaii in 1975. After the meeting, you walked around the venue, waving at and encouraging all of us staff members. When I saw you, I felt as if a brilliant sun had risen in my heart, and I realized that the source of all the warm, sincere encouragement I had received from my fellow members was you, our mentor.

IKEDA: Thank you for your kind words.

I'd like to take this opportunity to once again express my heartfelt appreciation to the members of our nurses groups and the doctors division, who always take care of first aid at various Soka Gakkai events.

Nothing Is Wasted in Soka Gakkai Activities

HAYASHI: After graduating from university, I understand that you got a job as a nurse at a university hospital, Ms. O'Connell. I've heard that it was your achievements there that led to your employment at San Francisco General Hospital.

O'CONNELL: That's correct. And when I started working at San Francisco General, I strove wholeheartedly to demonstrate proof of my faith there as well, especially since it was where I first encountered Buddhism. I chanted earnestly with a sincere prayer for the recovery of each patient and did my utmost to give them the very best care at all times. No matter how difficult the job that was given to me, I never refused it, and I always tried to keep a smile on my face, regardless of how hard it was.

MORITA: Where did you learn to have such an attitude toward your work?

O'CONNELL: It was completely due to my Soka Gakkai activities and President Ikeda's guidance. Everything I experienced through Soka Gakkai activities was useful. In particular, I learned to listen to others' problems and encourage them sincerely based on faith. Eventually, at work, whenever patients, other nurses, or even doctors had a problem, they would come to talk to me about it.

IKEDA: The Lotus Sutra has the beautiful phrase: "Breezes scented with sandalwood delight the hearts of the assembly" (LSOC, 39). Sincere behavior creates an atmosphere of trust that spreads like the refreshing scent of sandalwood. As President Makiguchi said, being victorious means shining as an indispensable person.

Knowing the Hospital Better Than Anyone

MORITA: Having earned the trust of your colleagues, you were recommended for the position of director of the hospital's Department of Education, Training, and Research. From there, you became director of nursing, with full responsibility for the nursing department, and then chief operations officer, in charge of overseeing all departments. Finally, eight years ago (in 1998), you were promoted to CEO.

O'CONNELL: Usually my post is occupied by a business executive with strong business acumen, or by an eminent physician. But the city of San Francisco, which selects the person for this position, gave me its full support.

IKEDA: You are one of the first women and nurses to become the CEO of a major hospital in the United States. What factors do you believe played a decisive role in your appointment?

O'CONNELL: I heard that one was that I knew the hospital better than anyone else.

IKEDA: I see! It's certainly true that a good nurse is the first to accurately grasp a patient's condition.

MORITA: Yes. I don't think it's an exaggeration to say that a doctor's effectiveness depends upon the nurse in charge.

IKEDA: It follows, then, that a hospital with excellent nurses is an excellent hospital.

MORITA: Yes, I think the quality of the nursing staff is a very important factor in evaluating a hospital.

Mutual Respect Gives Rise to Unity

HAYASHI: Good hospitals are those where doctors and nurses have mutual trust and function as a team. Regular and thorough communication between doctors and nurses is crucial. A lack of communication leads to medical errors.

IKEDA: Unity is vital to the growth and success of any organization. As Nichiren says, "If the spirit of many in body but one in mind prevails among the people, they will achieve all their goals, whereas if one in body but different in mind, they can achieve nothing remarkable" (WND-1, 618). This is an unchanging rule.

MORITA: For example, a detailed report written by nurses working the night shift can be of tremendous use to doctors making their rounds the following day.

HAYASHI: It's also encouraging for nurses if doctors take the time to acknowledge their labors; for instance, by thanking them in advance for their efforts on the night shift.

O'CONNELL: Creating teamwork requires mutual respect and the sharing of knowledge and information among colleagues. Physicians are experts in their field, and nurses have a great deal of vital information that they acquire through their daily contact with patients. Nurses have a duty to report the patients' constantly changing conditions to physicians, and it is the physicians' responsibility to listen to those reports.

IKEDA: Genuine unity is born from a shared goal and mutual respect. Doctors alone don't treat patients. True patient care is achieved through the combined efforts of everyone involved—including nurses, technicians, pharmacists, and hospital administrative staff. Each member of the team is indispensable.

Doctors and Nurses Are Equals Working Together

O'Connell: There are of course some hard-to-please doctors whom nurses have a difficult time with!

Ikeda: Nurses and doctors are human. Both have their own lives filled with various problems separate from their work. As a result, they may behave emotionally or irrationally on occasion. It's at such times, however, that both doctors and nurses need to return to their starting point and remember that patients come first.

Additionally, doctors mustn't be treated as superior to nurses. Writing to the Ikegami brothers, who were facing a plot to destroy their unity, Nichiren says, "The fact that the two of you are one in mind may be likened to the two wheels of a carriage, or the two wings of a bird" (WND-2, 914). The same applies to doctors and nurses. In a sense, doctors are dedicated to curing while nurses are dedicated to caring. Committed to the mutual goal of protecting patients' lives, they must therefore work together as partners, as colleagues, as collaborators, functioning like the two wheels of a cart.

Morita: It is even said that nurses are more important than doctors. As such, it is absolutely unacceptable for doctors to treat nurses like their subordinates.

Ikeda: In any case, nurses must be treasured and cherished above all. The great Japanese writer Sōseki Natsume (1867–1916) was frequently hospitalized with ulcers, and he never failed to treat his nurses with the highest respect. He was careful to learn their names and always addressed them politely—just what you would expect of a figure like Soseki.

HAYASHI: Nurses deeply appreciate that kind of consideration.

IKEDA: Ms. O'Connell, as the CEO of a hospital, what do you regard as the most important factor for the institution's growth?

O'CONNELL: My main concern is how we can provide our patients with the services they need. I also make an effort to encourage, inspire, and support everyone involved in patient care to develop an awareness that our sole function is to serve the patients first and foremost, as you mentioned earlier.

IKEDA: I really admire your conviction. We must never forget the purpose of institutions and whom they are meant to serve.

Wisdom Is Found on the Front Lines

IKEDA: Unfortunately, cases of medical malpractice have been increasing in Japan in recent years and they are becoming a serious social issue. What measures do you all suggest for preventing medical malpractice?

O'CONNELL: In the hospital I work for, we have set up a special committee whose sole function is to consider what can be done to ensure the safety of every patient.

MORITA: It is also very important to share information about accidents that were narrowly averted. Anyone can make a mistake. By sharing information about errors or close calls, we can encourage one another's prudence and implement measures to prevent new mistakes from happening.

HAYASHI: One of my nursing seniors taught me about this using the analogy of cheese. People are like Swiss cheese, filled with holes, she said. We all have shortcomings or weaknesses, and these can become the cause of mistakes. But when you pile slices of Swiss cheese on top of one another, the chances of a single hole going all the way through the stack is very low. In the same way, when several people work together, the likelihood of an error occurring is greatly reduced.

IKEDA: In other words, it's important to ask everyone's opinion, identify as many potential problems as possible, and pool everyone's wisdom. That's the way to successfully avoid accidents. Toward that end, the parties involved must discuss matters face to face, examining the issues promptly and carefully. Acting without consulting others or shirking one's responsibility only leads to trouble.

O'CONNELL: Our hospital has a supervisory team of which I am a member. We meet directly not only with doctors and nurses but with everyone working on the front lines of the hospital, including the janitorial staff, and discuss how we can make the hospital a safer, better place for patients.

IKEDA: That's a very important system. The wisdom to solve problems can always be found among those working on the front lines.

Reverence for Life Is the Foundation for Safety

MORITA: Perhaps the most basic cause of medical malpractice is when doctors or nurses occasionally forget the fundamental philosophy of reverence for life.

O'CONNELL: That must never be allowed to happen. A spirit of true service and commitment to patients also derives from a life-affirming philosophy. This should be the basis of every person involved in the practice of medicine.

IKEDA: I have heard it said that there are three requirements in medical treatment: skill, a spirit of service, and prayer. Indispensable to all of these, I believe, is a correct view of life. Having a firm philosophy enables one to fully utilize one's skills, deepens one's spirit of service to others, and gives power to one's prayers. Only then is treatment that places the patient first truly possible.

Nichiren says, "Life is the foremost of all treasures" (WND-1, 1125). Today, when our safety and security seem threatened on so many fronts, we need to return to the fundamental starting point of respect for the sanctity of life. Reevaluating everything from that perspective, let us continue moving forward, making safety and no accidents our top priority.

10: The Human Touch

Dialogue and Encouragement as Sources of Healing

Ikeda: I'd like to present a poem to the members of the Shirakaba nurses groups in Japan as well as our members working in the nursing field around the world, with my prayers for their happiness:

> *Members of our nurses groups*
> *in your beautiful white uniforms—*
> *how admirable you are*
> *in your dedication*
> *to protect life.*

Hayashi: Thank you! That is wonderful encouragement for us all.

O'Connell: Thank you very much! President Ikeda, you have frequently lauded the essential spirit of nurses, starting with Florence Nightingale.

Ikeda: Nightingale firmly believed that nothing could be achieved without effort. How noble are the efforts all of our nurses are making day and night. Without a doubt, their lives will be adorned with the brilliant laurels of victory.

O'Connell: Florence Nightingale, who devoted herself tirelessly to caring for wounded soldiers, was called the "lady of the lamp." The nurses of the Shirakaba groups and in fact all Soka women are also illuminating the lives of many with the "lamp of hope."

Ikeda: Ms. Hayashi, your mother, Eiko Hayashi, was truly a Florence Nightingale of kosen-rufu. I am overjoyed that you have inherited her spirit and are following in her footsteps.

Hayashi: Thank you. I owe everything to the kind support of you and Mrs. Ikeda.

Morita: Our readers have commented that they were very moved to hear Ms. O'Connell's experience and expressed a wish to also hear the story of Ms. Hayashi's mother.

O'Connell: Yes, I would also like to know more about the life of that wonderful senior in faith and nursing.

Hayashi: My mother took a leave of absence from her job as a nurse when I was born. Just as she was planning to return, when I was in the second grade at Tokyo Soka Elementary School, she was diagnosed with cancer.

Morita: She had an extremely rare form of cancer, a malignant melanoma in her large intestine.

Protected by the Positive Forces of the Universe

Ikeda: I believe that was at the end of 1984. I received the news that Eiko had been admitted to Keio University Hospital, which is very close to the Soka Gakkai Headquarters. My wife and I immediately began to pray earnestly for her recovery.

HAYASHI: My mother was told she had only three months to live. Since there was nothing more medically that could be done for her, she was allowed to spend her remaining days at home. She stayed undaunted through all of this.

IKEDA: I understand that she continued to read Nichiren's writings every morning and evening, and that there was one passage from "On Practicing the Buddha's Teachings" that she took especially to heart:

> As long as we are alive, we must keep chanting Nam-myoho-renge-kyo, Nam-myoho-renge-kyo. Then, if we chant until the very moment of death, Shakyamuni, Many Treasures, and the Buddhas of the ten directions will come to us instantly, exactly as they promised during the ceremony at Eagle Peak. Taking our hands and bearing us on their shoulders, they will carry us to Eagle Peak. (WND-1, 395)

That's why she wasn't worried or afraid. She brimmed with courage and conviction based on these words. Nichiren's writings are the source of strength that enable us to transform the sufferings of birth, aging, sickness, and death into the hope of eternity, happiness, true self, and purity.

HAYASHI: My father, brother, and I received encouragement from you on numerous occasions during my mother's illness. This taught me the importance of also encouraging the family members of people struggling with illness.

IKEDA: I'm sure you and your brother were never out of your mother's thoughts. I could imagine her feelings all too well and wanted to do whatever I could to encourage both of you throughout that difficult time.

Our Loved Ones Live On in Our Hearts

HAYASHI: My mother died on July 16, 1985. That morning, my brother and I went to see her at the hospital, to which she had been readmitted, before we left for school. I'll never forget her smile as she held our hands and said goodbye to us.

MORITA: That afternoon, while having her hands washed and her nails clipped by a nurse as she waited to be examined, Eiko Hayashi peacefully passed away.

IKEDA: When I visited the Tokyo Soka Elementary School the next day for a school event, I called you and your brother to my side and spoke with you.

HAYASHI: You said to us: "Your mother is always here. She will always be alive in your hearts, so you have nothing to worry about. You can think of my wife as your mother and me as your father. You have two fathers now." Though I was just a little girl, I still remember as if it were yesterday how touched I was by your kindness.

IKEDA: There are many people like you who have lost parents when they were young. But this has a profound significance from a Buddhist perspective. Buddhism teaches that life and death are indivisible. Therefore, when the children of a deceased person lead victorious, hope-filled lives, it means that the deceased, too, has triumphed.

Noting how her deceased husband was probably longing to hear news of their small children, Nichiren encouraged the lay nun Myoshin, "Because you are always chanting the daimoku of the Lotus Sutra, the character *myo* will change into an emissary to your husband . . . [who will] report all the affairs of your family in the saha world to [him]" (WND-2, 879).

Just as invisible radio and light waves can reach the moon and stars, strong resolve based on the Mystic Law communicates instantly over vast distances. It isn't limited to the present, either, but can even reach the lives of those who have passed away. That's why, though we may be physically separated from our loved ones, our hearts are always together and connected.

O'CONNELL: Nichiren's words are very profound.

IKEDA: I hope everyone who has lost a loved one will live out their lives with strength and optimism, firmly convinced that through the power of the Mystic Law, the deceased will quickly be reborn close by.

Brimming With Hope in Lifetime After Lifetime

MORITA: Life is eternal. Death is like our going to sleep at night.

IKEDA: That's right. One day in his later years, the German writer Johann Wolfgang von Goethe remarked to his friend as they admired the setting sun, "Still it continues the self-same sun, e'en while it is sinking."[45] It was a quote from ancient times, and Goethe went on to compare human life to the sun. The sun does not die or disappear when it sets. Though it sinks below the horizon out of sight, it continues to shine brightly. Goethe commented, "[The thought of death] never gives me uneasiness; for I am convinced that our spirit is indestructible, and that its activity continues from eternity to eternity."[46]

O'CONNELL: This view of life expressed by Goethe seems very similar to the Buddhist view of life's eternity across the three existences of past, present, and future.

IKEDA: Yes, it is. Those who have dedicated their lives to kosen-rufu will without a doubt experience a magnificent death, like the setting sun illuminating the sky with its golden glow. And just as a beautiful sunset promises fine weather come dawn, it is guaranteed that such people will enjoy a life brimming with hope and good fortune in lifetime after lifetime.

O'CONNELL: The philosophy of savoring joy in both life and death that you spoke of during a lecture at Harvard University shines with ever greater wisdom as time passes.

STRENGTHENING HUMAN TIES

IKEDA: Thank you.

To change the subject a bit, I would like to ask each of you what you think is most important in your interaction with patients.

MORITA: For me, the first thing is to relieve their anxiety.

IKEDA: It's certainly true that when you are ill you are constantly struggling with anxiety. So the challenge is to alleviate your patient's fears and give them hope. This is like the Buddhist teaching of "relieving suffering and imparting joy."

MORITA: In the case of terminal cancer patients, in particular, anxiety can intensify their pain. There seems to be a strong relationship between pain and anxiety.

IKEDA: Yes, that makes sense. So what can you do to relieve anxiety?

HAYASHI: I think the first step is to build a trusting relationship with the patient. Only when you have that can treatment be genuinely effective.

IKEDA: Dr. René Simard, the renowned cancer expert, once commented to me that the very existence of communication between physician and patient aids in healing. But, he lamented, at present the medical profession is dominated by technology, with less and less importance being placed on the doctor-patient relationship.[47]

MORITA: I once heard from a patient about a doctor who was so preoccupied with filling in his patient's computerized chart on his computer that he never even glanced up from the screen to look at the man. Finally the patient said in disgust, "But doctor, you haven't even examined me!" With a look of resignation, the doctor finally put his stethoscope to the patient's chest—but it wasn't the stethoscope at all. It was his computer mouse!

IKEDA: Dr. Simard was concerned that an overreliance on medical technology would destroy the human bond between doctor and patient. But he found hope in the fact that more and more women were entering the medical profession, expressing his belief that women's generally superior communication skills would strengthen the doctor-patient dialogue.

THE VOICE DOES THE BUDDHA'S WORK

HAYASHI: I think the basis for creating trust with our patients is our sincere wish for them to get well. Warm encouragement is also important, because it ignites the flame of hope in their hearts.

O'CONNELL: I have experience caring for a terminal cancer patient myself. She was very difficult and no one else wanted to help her. But with the thought that part of my job was to give her hope, I continued to encourage her, assuring her that she'd recover and that there were others whose symptoms were much more severe. Though I knew she might find me a nuisance, I would visit her every morning and say, "You're going to get better!" She eventually opened up to me and in the end, she left the hospital and became an outpatient.

IKEDA: "The voice carries out the work of the Buddha" (OTT, 4). Indeed, the voice is very powerful. We can be constantly thinking of another person, but if we don't say anything, they'll never know. It's important to put our thoughts into words and communicate them clearly. Nichiren writes, "Words echo the thoughts of the mind and find expression through the voice" (WND-2, 843).

I'm sure that when you energetically convey to your patients your wish to do whatever you can for them and your desire for them to get well, your sincerity and the warmth of your voice become a tremendous source of strength that can help them on the road to recovery.

MORITA: That's true. Sincere, warmhearted encouragement can improve a medicine's efficacy and can help alleviate pain better than morphine.

The Power of Words

HAYASHI: Depending on how we say something, our words can sound either like encouragement or like an order. For example, when we want a patient to take their medication, instead of just telling them they have to do so, we can suggest it in a kind and friendly way.

MORITA: When a patient asks whether they have a chance of recovery from a serious illness, some doctors reply that there is no known cure at present, while others put it in a more positive way, saying that leading specialists around the world are working on finding a cure right now.

IKEDA: My friend, the late Norman Cousins (1915–90), once said: "Words are weapons or building blocks, especially when used by a physician. They can set the stage for auspicious treatment or they can complicate and retard it."[48] The way doctors phrase their thoughts can have a major effect on patients. Patients usually have great respect for their doctors, so it can affect them deeply if their doctors are rude or unfeeling toward them.

MORITA: Unfortunately, there are arrogant people in the medical profession as well as those who are flippant and sarcastic or who make inappropriate and unprofessional comments to their patients. But this is just the kind of behavior that doctors should avoid at all costs.

The Doctor-Patient Relationship

O'CONNELL: One of the best ways to relieve patients' anxieties is for medical professionals to provide patients with a clear and full explanation of their condition and treatment. I think doctors who realize that different patients have different levels of understanding when it comes to such explanations and respond accordingly are ones who can be trusted.

IKEDA: The attitude that patients don't need to know all the facts and should just silently obey their doctor is hopelessly outdated. The age when doctors were the boss and patients passively did as they were told is over.

MORITA: I agree. A new doctor-patient relationship, in which patients are the main protagonists and doctors play a supporting role, is needed.

IKEDA: In that regard, patients can no longer just leave everything up to the doctor, either. The reality, however, is that many people take their doctor's words as divine pronouncements. I'm reminded of the remarks of Dr. Unger, who pointed out that the word *minister* originally meant *to serve*. It is thus the physician's role to serve their patients, he said, adding that both government and medicine should be arts of serving the people.

O'CONNELL: Florence Nightingale fearlessly took on anyone in her efforts to get the best care for patients; it didn't matter whether they were a doctor or a person in authority. Her patients were her number one priority.

MORITA: We need to see a fundamental transformation in consciousness take place in every field of human endeavor so that people become the main focus.

IKEDA: A Buddhist scripture urges people who are ill to take the positive approach of continuing to make efforts to get well and to bring out their wisdom.[49] This, too, emphasizes the importance of patients playing an active role in their recovery.

MORITA: We are inundated with health information today—on television, in magazines, and in many other media. People need the wisdom to distinguish the good information from the bad.

HAYASHI: Now is a time when patients are choosing their doctors. If they are unsatisfied with an explanation they've received, they can seek a second opinion from someone else.

The Power of Daimoku to Create Unlimited Hope

IKEDA: Is there anything else that you pay special attention to in your interaction with patients?

HAYASHI: Being hospitalized for a long time takes a toll mentally and emotionally on patients, and it is easy for them to become depressed. I am always chanting for a way to give such patients hope and lift their spirits. Before I enter their hospital room or have any interaction with them, whether it be giving them an injection or rubbing their hand to comfort them, I chant earnestly in my heart for their happiness.

O'CONNELL: When I was an active nurse, I also used to chant each morning that all my patients would receive the best care possible. I continue to chant for all the patients in our hospital every day.

IKEDA: The Mystic Law is the most beneficial medicine there is. It enables us to limitlessly tap and amplify the hope that everyone has deep inside. Since body and mind are inseparable, the hope that we bring forth is certain to have a positive effect on our physical being as well.

HAYASHI: That's very true. I once cared for a woman who was in her forties and had breast cancer. She had a tumor in her left breast removed, but the cancer spread to her lungs. This setback didn't discourage her, however. She was always smiling, determined that as long as she had faith, she would never be defeated. She chanted softly to herself, taking care not to disturb others in her hospital room. Gradually more and more patients, impressed by her example, expressed a wish to be in the same ward or room with her.

IKEDA: People naturally gravitate to those who are positive and upbeat. No doubt the other patients were drawn to her by the philosophy of hope found in Nichiren Buddhism that she was a vibrant example of. What became of her?

HAYASHI: She needed additional surgery, but the tumor in her lungs was large and she still had adhesions from the first operation, so the doctor in charge decided it was too risky. With numerous chemotherapy treatments, however, her tumor shrunk and she asked to have the second operation. But her doctor remained opposed. He said that the cancer could well have metastasized to her lymph nodes, so surgery would probably be useless anyway. No matter how hard she prayed, he said, there was no hope.

Still, she insisted on having the surgery. It turned out that the cancer had not spread to her lymph nodes and the surgery was a success. No one was more astonished than her doctor, who admitted that the power of belief was truly a wondrous thing. Her example completely changed his attitude toward the positive role that religious faith can play.

The Effect of Faith on Healing

Morita: The *Seikyo Shimbun* once carried an interview with a psychoimmunologist who spoke about what are sometimes considered "miraculous recoveries." He said that the spiritual activity of prayer can have a positive effect on the immune system that medical science cannot quantify.

Ikeda: Yes, that's very true. President Toda's doctor actually said the same thing, stating that Mr. Toda's recovery was a clear indication of the power of faith that couldn't be explained by medical science. He also expressed his astonishment at the strength of Mr. Toda's life force. The situation was that about six months before he passed away, President Toda grew very weak and his condition became very serious. But a month later, he took a turn for the better and within three months he was showing signs of a full recovery.

Mr. Toda told his doctor that the devil of illness that afflicted him was a little one, adding that it was only natural that such an obstacle would appear after he had attained the momentous goal of 750,000 households.[50] If he was defeated by this illness, he said, kosen-rufu would never be accomplished.

O'Connell: What a vigorous spirit he had!

Ikeda: The flame of kosen-rufu was always burning brightly in President Toda's heart. I'm sure his fighting spirit gave him the power to conquer the devil of illness. When we pray and struggle to realize kosen-rufu, indomitable strength wells forth from the depths of our being. We can tap inexhaustible life force and hope, and manifest a "jeweled sword" of courage to surmount the devil of illness.

Nichikan (1665–1726), who is known as a great restorer of Nichiren Buddhism, wrote, "Through the power of the Mystic Law, we manifest the life of the Daishonin within ourselves."[51] This is the ultimate essence of faith. We manifest Nichiren's life force in our own lives and can take on any struggle with the same strength. As a result, there is no illness that can defeat us. We cannot fail to attain happiness. Our lives will in fact be enriched through facing illness. With such conviction, let's live out our lives with optimism and dignity as we walk the great path of eternity, happiness, true self, and purity!

Notes

CHAPTER 1: LEARNING FROM ILLNESS
1. Linus Pauling and Daisaku Ikeda, *A Lifelong Quest for Peace: A Dialogue,* trans. Richard L. Gage (Boston: Jones and Bartlett Publishers, 1992), 45.
2. At the time of this dialogue, Dr. Shosaku Narumi was the Soka Youth Physicians Conference Chair.
3. At the time of this dialogue, Dr. Chiaki Nishiyama was the Soka Gakkai Doctors Division Women's Leader.
4. At the time of this dialogue, Dr. Yochi Uehigashi was the Soka Gakkai Tokyo Doctors Division Secretary.
5. *Buddhist Legends,* trans. Eugene Watson Burlingame (London: Pali Text Society, 1969), 258–59. This is a translation from the original Pali text of the *Dhammapada Commentary.*
6. See *The Sutra of the Wise and the Foolish* or *The Ocean of Narratives,* trans. Stanley Frye (New Delhi: Library of Tibetan Works & Archives, 1981), 64–65.
7. *The Yellow Emperor's Classic of Medicine: A New Translation of the Neijing Suwen with Commentary,* trans. Maoshing Ni (Boston: Shambhala Publications, Inc., 1995), 158.
8. Romain Rolland, *Jean-Christophe in Paris,* trans. Gilbert Cannan (New York: Henry Holt and Company, 1911), 183.
9. Viktor E. Frankl, *The Doctor and the Soul,* trans. Richard and Clara Winston (New York: Alfred A. Knopf, 1968), 109.

CHAPTER 2: BUDDHISM AND MEDICINE
10. Plutarch, *Plutarch's Morals,* trans. from the Greek by several hands, corrected and revised by William W. Goodwin (Boston: Little, Brown, and Company, 1874), 265–66.
11. Daisaku Ikeda, René Simard, and Guy Bourgeault, *On Being Human: Where Ethics, Medicine, and Spirituality Converge* (Santa Monica, CA: Middleway Press, 2003), 52.

Chapter 3: The Influenza Mystery
12. Daisaku Ikeda, *My Dear Friends in America*, Third Edition (Santa Monica, CA: World Tribune Press, 2012), 336–49.
13. Spanish flu: Some studies estimate the deaths at between 50 and 100 million.

Chapter 4: Are Our Lives Determined by Our Genes?
14. The Contemplation on the Mind-Ground Sutra.
15. As of 2014, evidence suggests that there are nineteen thousand to twenty thousand protein-coding genes in the human genome.
16. Florence Nightingale, *Notes on Nursing: What It Is, and What It Is Not* (New York: Dover Publications, Inc., 1969), 8.
17. Stephen Jay Gould, *The Mismeasure of Man* (New York: W. W. Norton & Company, 1996), 369–70.
18. *The Diamond Scalpel:* A work by Miao-lo that maintains that even insentient beings are endowed with the potential for Buddhahood.

Chapter 5: Children and Stress
19. According to the December 22, 2005, edition of the Japanese daily *Yomiuri Shimbun*, the number of hospitals with pediatrics departments continues to decline in Japan, down 22 percent from its peak in 1990.
20. The English edition of SGI President Ikeda's dialogue with Dr. Ved Nanda, "Our World to Make," was published in 2015.
21. Ved Nanda and Daisaku Ikeda, *Our World to Make* (Cambridge, MA: Dialogue Path Press, 2015), 8.

Chapter 6: A Constructive Approach to Aging
22. This dialogue took place in February 2006.
23. Seneca, *Ad Lucilium, Epistulae Morales*, in *Seneca in Ten Volumes*, trans. Richard M. Gummere (Cambridge, MA: Harvard University Press, 1989), 4:67.
24. Inazo Nitobe, *The Works of Inazo Nitobe* (Tokyo: University of Tokyo Press, 1972), 5:122.
25. Ikeda, Simard, and Bourgeault, *On Being Human*, 73–74.
26. André Maurois, *The Art of Living,* trans. James Whitall (London: Penguin Books, 1960), 180.
27. Serge Bramly, *Leonardo: The Artist and the Man,* trans. Sian Reynolds (London: Penguin Books, 1991), 401.
28. Ralph Waldo Emerson, *Essays and Lectures* (New York: Library of America, 1983), 57.

Chapter 7: "We Will Find Perpetual Youth"

29. George Sand, *The Story of My Life*, a group translation, ed. Thelma Jurgrau (Albany, NY: State University of New York Press, 1991), 1:595.
30. Fang Zhaoling passed away on February 20, 2006, after this dialogue took place.
31. Victor Hugo, *Les Misérables,* trans. Lee Fahnestock and Norman MacAfee (New York: New American Library, 1987), 1337.
32. Daisaku Ikeda, "Mahayana Buddhism and Twenty-First-Century Civilization," *A New Humanism: The University Addresses of Daisaku Ikeda* (New York: Weatherhill, 1996), 152.
33. Walt Whitman, "Beautiful Women," *Leaves of Grass* (New York: Everyman's Library, 1968), 232.

Chapter 8: Dealing With Dementia

34. Johann Wolfgang von Goethe, *Conversations of Goethe with Johann Peter Eckermann,* trans. John Oxenford (New York: Da Capo Press, 1998), 101–102.
35. *The Ten Divisions of Monastic Rules.*
36. Thomas T. Perls and Margery Hutter Silver, *Living to 100: Lessons in Living to Your Maximum Potential at Any Age* (New York: Basic Books, 1999), 72.
37. Goethe, *Conversations of Goethe with Johann Peter Eckermann*, 354.
38. Maurois, *The Art of Living*, 180.
39. Translated from Japanese. Ekiken Kaibara, *Yojo kun, wazoku doji kun* (Lessons on Health and Education), ed. Ken Ishikawa (Tokyo: Iwanami Shoten, 1972), 159.
40. Jean-Jacques Rousseau, *Emile,* or *On Education,* trans. Allan Bloom (London: Penguin Books, 1991), 42.
41. SGI President Ikeda's dialogue with John Kenneth Galbraith was published in 2005, in Japanese; it is not available in English.
42. Lynn Peters Adler, *Centenarians: The Bonus Years* (Santa Fe, NM: Health Press, 1995), 17.

Chapter 9: The Key to Good Health Care

43. Dr. Morita was leader of the Soka Gakkai doctors division until November 2006, when he was appointed as the division's general leader.
44. Gene Marie O'Connell was CEO of San Francisco General Hospital until 2009.

Chapter 10: The Human Touch

45. Goethe, *Conversations of Goethe with Johann Peter Eckermann*, 60.

46. Ibid.
47. Ikeda, Simard, and Bourgeault, *On Being Human*, 57–58.
48. Norman Cousins, *The Healing Heart: Antidotes to Panic and Helplessness* (New York: W. W. Norton & Company, 1983), 112.
49. From the *Makasamghika Vinaya* (The Great Canon of Monastic Rules).
50. Josei Toda, determined to rebuild the Soka Gakkai after the end of World War II, set about to develop its membership from less than 3,000 families when he assumed the presidency in 1951 to more than 750,000 households before his death in 1958, thereby spreading the movement across Japan and throughout society. At the time of his death on April 2, 1958, the Soka Gakkai has exceeded 750,000 households.
51. From "Totaigi sho mondan" (Commentary on "The Entity of the Mystic Law").

Index

ability, increased by effort, 58
action, 74; prompt, 30
advancement, 24, 46, 83, 86, 94–95, 103
aging, abilities that improve with, 97–98; creating value to the process of, 102; facing, 74–82, 87, 89, 91–93, 95–97, 101, 105, 107, 116–17, 119, 121–22, 128
Aichi, doctors division of, 74
Ajatashatru, 7
alert, always be, 37
All-America General Meeting, Hawaii, 129
Alzheimer, Alois, 104
Alzheimer's disease, facing, 105–106, 114
appreciation, 52, 64, 109, 120, 125, 129
Ariyoshi, Sawako, 106–108
Ariyoshi, Tamao, 107
Athayde, Austregésilo de, 82, 85
Atsuta Village, 90
attitude, 92, 115–17, 128, 148–49

beauty, 99
benefit, 66
bodhisattva, spirit of the, 99–101, 129
Bodhisattva Medicine King, 19

Boey, Chiong Meng, 57–58, 61, 63, 66
Borisov, Andrei S., 25
Bourgeault, Guy, 24, 81–82
Brazilian Academy of Letters, 82
Buddha, the, as the king of physicians, 19
Buddhism, 3–4, 6, 12, 17, 24, 34, 41, 46, 66, 76, 79, 94, 97, 115–16, 148; and medicine, 19–21; practitioners of, 55; promoting, 94, 113, 127; and the universe, 54

Caecus, Appius Claudius, 46
carelessness, 36
Casals, Pablo, 94
cause and effect, Buddhist law of, 45
challenge, spirit of, 24, 81, 93–94, 120, 130
children, actions and words used against, 61–62; and the future of humanity, 59; parents relationship with, 60–63
Chinese University of Hong Kong, 38
commitment, 37, 87
communications, 132
community, relations with, 6, 58, 64, 73, 100–101, 118, 120

compassion, 6, 30, 42, 51, 69, 117;
  Buddhist spirit of, 40, 52, 60
consent, winning one's, 110
courage, 11, 25, 30, 69, 71, 92, 139,
  150
Cousins, Norman, 145
creativity, 92
crisis, precaution against a, 37–38
curiosity, 120

daimoku (Nam-myoho-renge-
  kyo), chanting, 141
death, 2; Buddhist perspective of,
  3, 33, 66–67, 69–71, 97, 122–23,
  139, 141; denial about, 32–33;
  facing, 30–31
dementia, facing, 104–105,
  107–13, 115, 120; preventing,
  117–18
determination, 11, 23, 37, 67, 71,
  81–82, 106, 114, 134, 139, 141,
  150
Devadatta, envy and arrogance
  of, 7–8
dialogue, 118, 143
diseases, genetic, 48
doctors, role of, 6–7, 59, 136
doctor-patient relationship, 6–7,
  42–43, 142–47
doctors, and nurses, 131
doctors division, 2, 5–7, 19, 69,
  126, 129
dynamism, spirit of, 86

education, humanistic, 30
efforts, 12, 43, 52, 137
elderly, interacting with the, 117;
  respecting the, 98–100; using
  the energy of the, 101

Emerson, Ralph Waldo, 86
empathy, feeling, 51
encouragement, importance of,
  7, 23, 30, 32, 42, 50–52, 67–70,
  113, 119, 126, 128, 130, 134,
  137, 139–41, 144
environment, role of the, 43
eternity of life, 66, 90, 141
European Academy of Sciences
  and Arts, 42
experiences, sharing, 101

family members, of the deceased,
  70, 139–41
Fang Zhaoling, 82, 93
Faust (Goethe), 93
fighting spirit, 24, 85, 87, 121–22;
  of Josei Toda, 149
fostering, capable individuals, 13,
  29, 80, 100
four elements, 17–18
four sufferings (birth, aging,
  sickness, and death), 2–3, 6–7;
  Buddhist view of, 4; transforming, 34, 41, 97, 139
four virtues (eternity, happiness,
  true self, and purity), 3, 13, 34,
  85, 97, 116, 150; savoring the,
  123
Frankl, Viktor E., 11–12
friendship, 114, 118
future, creating a better, 46, 101

Galbraith, John Kenneth, 121
genetics, 44–47; misuse of, 52–53
goal, 5–6, 82–83; shared, 132
Goethe, Johann Wolfgang von,
  93, 103, 117; life as viewed by,
  141–42

Gohonzon (object of devotion), 12, 16
gongyo (recitation of the sutra and chanting Nam-myoho-renge-kyo), 15
good circumstances, creating, 66, 103, 114, 142
goodness, 63
Gould, Stephen J., 54
government, role of, 146
Great Canon of Monastic Rules, The, 22
growth, 46, 62, 81, 120–21, 132

Hammer, Armand, 82, 114
happiness, 7, 12, 30, 33, 48, 54–55, 64, 68–69, 71, 73, 83, 95, 114, 123, 137, 147, 150
Harvard University, "Mahayana Buddhism and Twenty-First-Century Civilization" address at, 34, 96, 142
Hayashi, Eiko, 126, 138, 140
health, 1, 15–16, 21–24, 26–27, 64, 68, 71, 73, 79, 84–85, 87, 89–91, 113–14, 120, 123, 128–29, 147–48; model to maintaining, 118
hearts of others, opening the, 87
Hippocrates, 34
Hirasawa, Ryuto, 26
Hong Kong Soka Kindergarten, with its model sanitation education, 38
hope, 7, 12, 30, 42, 46, 51, 62, 69–70, 91–92, 103, 128, 140–41, 143–44, 147–48, 150; philosophy of, 127
Hoyle, Fred, 4

Hugo, Victor, 96
human rights, 83, 85
humanism, 30

Illich, Ivan, 22
illness, facing, 9–13, 17–19, 21–24, 37–39, 67–69, 87, 95, 111, 128, 146–48, 150; family members facing, 139–41
inactivity, 86
Inamitsu, Reiko, 74
Influenza, 34–36; facing, 25–29
inner change, 146
inspiration, 92, 119–20, 134; to others, 103
intelligence, genetics and, 43–44
interactions, 117–18
Ishikawa no Hyoe, lay priest, 69

Jivaka (physician of Shakyamuni), 7–8
joy, 12, 71, 99, 116, 120, 123

Kaibara Ekiken, 118
Kant, Immanuel, 94
Katiyar, Sarvagya Singh, 48
Keio University Hospital, 74, 138
kosen-rufu, 68, 85, 113, 119, 123, 125, 138, 149; life dedicated to, 11, 71, 83, 87, 91, 114, 122, 142; Tsunesaburo Makiguchi's lead for, 113–14
Kurokawa, Nobuo, 64

Laboremus ("Let's get to work"; motto of Arnold J. Toynbee), 85
leaders, 30, 33, 126
learning, 121

Lee Jong-wook, 26
Leonardo, da Vinci, 86
Li, Arthur Kwok Cheung, 38
life, Buddhist view of, 12, 30, 34, 41, 66, 83–85, 87, 95, 118–19, 121–23, 135–36, 150
life and death, from a Buddhist perspective, 4, 140; joy in both, 69–71
life force, 12, 16, 21, 64, 67, 95, 116, 150
life span, 89; extending one's, 90–91
life state, 11, 40, 48, 95, 116
listening, importance of, 61, 80, 130, 132
longevity, 128
Lotus Sutra, 30, 86, 95, 99, 101, 116, 127, 130, 141

Makiguchi, Tsunesaburo, 21, 80, 94, 108, 130
malpractice, investigating medical, 65; preventing medical, 134–36
Many Treasures Group, 73; as a model organization, 83, 95, 101; members of the, 84, 100, 102
Matsuyama, Zenzo, 78
Maurois, Andre, 82
medicine, role of, 146
men's division, 64, 80
mentor-disciple relationship, 29, 44, 129; poem dedicated to the, 68
Michikawa, Makoto, 74
Miscellaneous Treasury Sutra, 99

mission, 58–59, 64, 70, 73, 82, 120–21, 128
Moses, Grandma, 94
myo, function of, 141
Myoichi (disciple of Nichiren), 50
Myoshin, lay nun, 141
Mystic Law, 12–13, 23, 141, 147–48, 150; life dedicated to the, 69, 73, 95, 97, 123, 127–28; as the highly effective medicine, 19

Nam-myoho-renge-kyo, chanting, 12, 15–16, 24, 34, 91, 116, 130, 139, 147–48
Nanda, Ved, 63
Nanjo Tokimitsu, 43, 67–70
National Institute for Longevity Sciences, Japan, 74
Natsume, Soseki, 133
neighing of white horses, metaphor for, 15
Newton, Isaac, 93
Nichikan, 150
Nichiren Daishonin, 10, 12, 15–17, 20–21, 23–24, 30, 32, 34, 40, 43, 50–52, 66–67, 69–70, 84, 87, 90, 95, 97, 98–100, 103, 109, 114–15, 118, 121–22, 127–28, 132–33, 136, 141, 144; genetic diseases as described by, 47; life state of, 68, 116; "On Practicing the Buddha's Teachings," 139; as the votary of the Lotus Sutra, 90; writings of, 92, 120, 139
Nightingale, Florence, 23, 49,

137–38; fearlessness of, 146; and patients, 146
Nitobe Inazo, 80
nurses, 137; respect for the, 133–34; role of, 134
nurses group, 19, 129

oneness of body and mind, 51
opinions, handling differences of, 117, 135
optimism, 71, 73, 141, 150
organizations, success of, 132

Pande, B.N., 82
Parallel Lives (Plutarch), 16
Parks, Rosa, 82
passion, 84, 87, 93
patients, visiting, 48–50
Pauling, Linus, 1, 82–83
people, creating a new age of the, 146
philosophy, 55
Plutarach, 16
praise, importance of giving, 52, 57, 62–63, 69
prayer, 24, 68, 130, 149
present moment, importance of the, 46, 76
Principia (Newton), 93
prosperity, 71, 98
Pugwash Conferences on Science and World Affairs, 54, 82

reading, importance of, 91–92, 115
Record of the Orally Transmitted Teachings, The, 34
relieving suffering and imparting joy, 142

religion, positive role of, 114, 148–49
respect, 62, 132
responsibility, sense of, 23, 37, 39, 120
role model, Jun Tokita as a, 84; young woman (Malaysia junior high school division member) as a, 66–69
Rolland, Romain, 10
Rotblat, Joseph, 82–83, 85
Rousseau, Jean-Jacques, 119

saha world, 115–16
Sairen-bo (disciple of Nichiren), 23
Sakha Republic (Yakutia), 25
San Francisco General Hospital, 125, 127, 129–31
Sand, George, 92
science, role of 54–55
Seikyo Shimbun, 149
self-confidence, 116
Seneca, 74
SGI, 125; members of the, 58, 127–28; publications of the, 92
Shakyamuni, 3, 7–8, 20, 29, 39, 99
Shichiro Goro (younger brother of Nanjo Tokimitsu), 71
Shijo Kingo, 20–21
Shin shujin zaitaku sutoresu shokogun (The New Retired Husband Syndrome) (Kurokawa), 64
Simard, René, 24, 143
sincerity, 128, 144
society, building a better, 6, 23, 33, 54–55, 59, 66, 73, 83–85, 99–101, 114, 119

Soeda, Asako, 121
Soka alumni, 6
Soka Gakkai, 33, 51, 66, 71, 78, 85–86, 94, 119; elderly members of the, 73; members of the, 11, 86–87; publications of the, 120
Soka Gakkai activities, 64, 84, 119–20, 130; as the best health regimen, 113–14
Soka Gakkai events, 129
Soka Gakkai Malaysia doctors division, 57
Soka High School, 5
Soka Kyoiku Gakkai (Value-Creating Education Society; forerunner of the Soka Gakkai), 94
Soka Tokyo Elementary school, 126, 138, 140
Soka University, 57, 68; correspondence education division of, the, 74, 121
Soka University of America (Calabasas campus), 83
spirituality, importance of, 86, 114
strength, 71, 99, 141, 149–50
stress, facing, 59–60; after retirement, 63–64
sufferings, transforming, 12, 24, 46, 115–16, 120, 127–28, 150
support, 134
sutra, reciting the, 91
Swaminathan, M.S., 54

Takamine, Hideko, 78
teachers, 59
teamwork, between doctors and nurses, 132–33

T'ien-t'ai, 17–18, 20; *Great Concentration and Insight*, 17
Toda, Josei, 8, 11, 21, 41, 44, 59, 85, 116, 121, 123
Tokai University Junior College of Nursing and Technology, 74
Toki, lay nun (wife of Toki Jonin), 109
Toki Jonin, 51
Tokita, Jun, 83, 85
Toynbee, Arnold J., 33, 82; motto of, 85
trust, 42, 57, 61–62, 130–31, 146
twenty-first century, creating a century of health and life in the, 1–2, 4, 13, 40, 55
Twilight Years, The (Ariyoshi), 106–107

understanding, 110
Unger, Felix, 42–43, 52, 65, 114, 146
unity, 132, 135; of Ikegami brothers (disciples of Nichiren Daishonin), 133
University of Denver, 63
University of Glasgow, 54
University of London, 81; Medical School, 58
University of Malaya, 58
University of Montreal, Canada, 24, 81

value, creating, 84
victory, 6, 71, 85, 91, 123, 130, 132, 137
vitality, 15, 46
voice, as a source of strength,

144–45; importance of using one's, 92
vow, 101

walking, exercise of, 113
water, drink plenty, 79
Whitman, Walt, 100
wisdom, 12, 22–23, 41, 54–55, 73, 92, 100–101, 116, 135, 142, 147
women, 126; and communication, 143; role of, 5
women's division, 128, 138
World Health Organization (WHO), 26

world peace, 83

Yomiuri Shimbun, 1
young women division Shirakaba Group (for those in the nursing profession), 74, 125–26, 128, 138; poem to the, 137
youth, hallmark of the, 81–83; life as a, 76, 78, 80
youthful spirit, 46, 81–82, 85, 87, 90, 93–95, 103, 120

Zhou Enlai, 107

Printed on recycled paper.

World Tribune Press is committed to preserving ancient forest and natural resources. We are a member of the Green Press Initiative—a nonprofit program dedicated to supporting book publishers in maximizing their use of fiber, which is not sourced from ancient or endangered forests. For this printing, we have elected to print this title on 55# Natures B19 Smooth Antique, 400 ppi, made with 30 percent post consumer waste, processed chlorine free.

For more information about the Green Press Initiative and the use of recycled paper in book publishing, visit www.greenpressinitiative.org